Britain's War Powers

Tara McCormack

Britain's War Powers

The Fall and Rise of Executive Authority?

palgrave
macmillan

Tara McCormack
School of History, Politics
and International Relations
University of Leicester
Leicester, UK

ISBN 978-3-030-13681-9 ISBN 978-3-030-13682-6 (eBook)
https://doi.org/10.1007/978-3-030-13682-6

Library of Congress Control Number: 2019936156

This Palgrave Pivot imprint is published by the registered company Springer Nature Switzerland AG
The registered company address is: Gewerbestrasse 11, 6330 Cham, Switzerland

Contents

CHAPTER 1

The Executive Strikes Back? The Rise and Fall of Britain's Parliamentary War Powers

Abstract The first part of the chapter sets out the main argument of the work: the Syria strikes of April 2018 suggest the new Parliamentary convention is weak to non-existent. This is fundamentally a problem of political will. The legislature failed in April 2018 to assert its rights even retrospectively. The fall and rise of the Royal Prerogative can be understood in the context of the declining authority of the executive *and* a legislature that does not wish to assert its own authority and ultimately that of the electorate. The work is then set in an academic context, that of the literature analysing the changing locus of British war powers. This literature is part of a larger field engaging with executive–legislative relations and foreign and security policy. The second part of the chapter gives an overview of the rest of the work and of the main arguments therein.

Keywords Royal prerogative · Parliamentary convention · Syria · Foreign policy · Security policy

Introduction

> How odd – perhaps bizarre – it is that the approval of both Houses of Parliament is required for pieces of technical, and often trivial, subordinate legislation, whereas it is not needed at all before men and women can be committed to the possibility of disfigurement or death. (Brazier 1999: 123)

T. McCormack, *Britain's War Powers*,
https://doi.org/10.1007/978-3-030-13682-6_1

'We must understand from previous conflicts that war is not some sort of hokey-cokey concept; once you're in, you're in…'. (Jim Sheridan, House of Commons, 29 August 2013, Debate and Motion Syria and the Use of Chemical Weapons, Hansard col 1447)

This work is an exploration of the brief rise and fall of what was considered to be a new Parliamentary convention on authorising war in Britain. The work was prompted by the British government's airstrikes against Syria in April 2018. The government refused to recall Parliament and also acted in the face of majority popular opposition to the action. Yet in the preceding five years it had been widely assumed that Parliamentary authority over war and conflict had been established, displacing the historic Royal Prerogative executive authority over war (Strong 2014; Mello 2017; Cabinet Office 2011).

The convention seemed to be established firmly in 2013, and then reaffirmed in 2015, when David Cameron went to Parliament to ask for authorisation for British airstrikes in Syria. In 2013, Parliament voted not to authorise airstrikes against the Syrian government in response to the use of chemical weapons. In 2015, Parliament voted to authorise British participation in coalition airstrikes against ISIS in Syria. Whilst it was the case that Parliamentary authority remained at the level of an (assumed) convention rather than on a statutory footing, and thus open to change, there was a widespread belief that the Conservative Prime Minister David Cameron's 'defeat' (Gaskarth 2016) in 2013 over intervention in Syria had established the convention. As Malcolm Chalmers the Deputy Director-General of the Royal United Services Institute (RUSI) commented after the 2013 vote:

> It is now hard to see how any UK Government could undertake significant military action without the support of Parliament, or indeed of the wider public. And it is difficult to see such support being given unless there is a clear national interest involved, or if military operations are undertaken with the imprimatur of a UN Security Council (UNSC) mandate - at least until the shadows of Iraq and Afghanistan have faded much further from the national consciousness. (Chalmers 2013)

Yet in April 2018, when faced with exactly the same circumstances as Cameron in 2013 and proposing exactly the same action, Theresa May chose not to ask Parliament for authorisation. May did not repudiate the convention, rather, May argued that the military action did not meet the criteria for the Parliamentary convention. However, the justifications given by her government do not stand up to scrutiny. Moreover, this was a military intervention in a highly precarious and tense situation that could have resulted in a much broader conflict. This work considers what happened and what the implications are for the Parliamentary convention.

What then has happened to the Parliamentary convention? Has the executive reasserted its power over the legislature? At the core of the book is a concern with fundamental questions of legitimate authority when it comes to potentially existential policy questions. Who *should* have the right to decide on war and peace? This is both a normative question, who in principle *should* have the authority, but also a particularly pertinent political question for post-Cold War Britain. Successive governments of different political persuasions have engaged in 'wars of choice' and the consequences of these wars are still central to international and domestic politics today. The question of legislative–executive relations and foreign policy is one that is fundamentally an issue of democracy and legitimacy. Foreign policy decisions of war and peace are ultimately political and moral decisions.

Moreover, successive post-Cold War British governments have a history of being less than scrupulous when it comes to making the case for military interventions and foreign policy. In the case of the Iraq war, it is an established fact that the Labour government led by Tony Blair actively misled the public as to the case for war (for example, see The Iraq Inquiry 2016, commonly known as the Chilcot Report after the Chair John Chilcot). Astonishingly, this catastrophic intervention and ensuing war that resulted in the loss of life of hundreds of thousands of people and created ongoing chaos in the Middle East is now being treated as an 'English disagreement' with warnings that we should not 'overlearn' the lessons of Iraq (*Financial Times* 2013). The Libyan intervention too was premised upon a case that was weak and, to put it charitably, was 'over-sold' by David Cameron (House of Commons 2016). The most recent Intelligence and Security Committee (ISC) report on Britain's role in secret rendition demonstrates an alarming degree of dishonesty from Labour *and* Conservative governments when it comes to foreign policy (Intelligence and Security Committee 2018).

A concern about declining legitimacy and therefore the question of legitimate authority was one of the main drivers behind the development of the new Parliamentary convention. It was broadly felt that in a situation of declining legitimacy and trust, serious constitutional changes and/or major political decisions should be authorised by Parliament, and by extension the electorate (this will be discussed detail in this chapter). Conversely, a sense of weakness and uncertainty has also led the current government to retreat from the new Parliamentary convention for fear that Parliament would not support the executive decision. But Parliament itself does not seem to wish to assert it's own authority, and more importantly, *our* authority, over the executive.

If in the space of four years two Prime Ministers, of the same political party, can respond in diametrically opposed ways to similar circumstances, it can reasonably be argued that the new Parliamentary convention is weak to the point of non-existence. May has learnt an important lesson from Cameron's requests for democratic authorisation from the electorate whether on bombing Syria or leaving the European Union; when you ask for democratic authorisation for a political policy the answer may not be the one that you want. If the convention can simply be ignored, if the government of the day worries the answer will be 'wrong', then it does not exist.

However, it will be argued that rather than a strong executive driving rough shod over Parliament, it was Parliament itself that did not assert itself and hold the executive to account. The legislature failed in April 2018 to assert Parliamentary rights even retrospectively. The fall and rise of the Royal Prerogative can be understood in the context of the declining authority of the executive *and* a weak legislature that does not wish to assert its own authority and ultimately that of the electorate.

Thus this work concludes somewhat differently than my initial thoughts at the start. I had thought to confidently argue for greater formalisation of the convention (which argument will still be made) but the problem is deeper. Whether convention or written constitution, or statute, legislative authority over and control of the executive is at its heart a political matter. Without the political will to enforce its own dominance, Parliamentary sovereignty is of little account. Moreover, Parliament in Britain, and in other representative democracies, is but a conduit for the expressed will of the citizens. When it comes to foreign and security policy post-Cold War, the British government has played a far more belligerent role than British public opinion supports. Thus Parliament is failing in its duty to hold the executive to account on our behalf.

This introductory chapter proceeds as follows. First of all, the work is set in an academic context, that of an existing body of literature analysing the changing locus of what are often called war powers in the British political system. This literature is part of a larger field of work that has emerged post-Cold War that engages with executive–legislative relations and foreign and security policy. The chapter then gives an overview of the rest of the work and of the main arguments therein.

War Powers and the Changing Relationship Between the Executive and the Legislature in Democratic States

In Britain, the power and authority to declare war has historically been an executive power (Strong 2014; Payne 2008). Following on from the Iraq war that began in 2003 the question of authorisation of war became an important political, constitutional and academic discussion; (for example Payne 2008; Blick 2014; Strong 2014, 2018; McCormack 2016; Gaskarth 2016; Kaarbo and Kenealy 2016; Mello 2017; Kaarbo 2018; Fikfak and Hooper 2018; House of Commons 2004; House of Lords 2006).

The discussion of Britain's war powers is a part of a wider body of work that engages with the changing locus of war powers in democratic states. The phrase war powers, although commonly used, does not fully capture what this work is engaging with. Any study of war powers is a study of various aspects of executive–legislative relations in relationship to foreign and security policy (Raunio and Wagner 2017: 2). The term war powers is also perhaps a little misleading. As has been noted by the House of Lords, declarations of war are virtually unheard of post-WWII (House of Lords 2006: 7). International law now more generally refers to 'armed conflict' (Joseph 2013). How to even describe what it is that may be authorised has been an important part of the academic and policy discussion in Britain and in other states (Ziegler 2019; House of Commons 2004: 9–10; also see McCormack 2016 for what is excluded). It is notable that Theresa May has interpreted the new Parliamentary convention as only being relevant for a very specific type of military action (as will be discussed).

The term war powers can also imply a specific statutory instrument but there are a number of ways in which legislatures can in principle hold executives to account in foreign policy (Mello and Peters 2018: 6; Rosén and Raube 2018). This is why the slightly more cumbersome but more explanatory phrases of 'executive-legislative relations and foreign and security policy' is a better expression of the body of work. This growing body of work focuses on different states, asks different questions and uses different methodologies (e.g. Wagner et al. 2010; Kesgin and Kaarbo 2010; Schuster and Maier 2006; Strong 2014, 2018; McCormack 2016; Lagasse and Saideman 2017; Herbel 2016; Hegemann 2018; Raunio 2016, 2018; Kaarbo 2018; Raunio and Wagner 2017; Wagner 2018; Wagner et al. 2017; Lagassé 2017). It is, as Mello and Peters argue in a very recent British Journal of Politics and IR special issue on the topic, an emerging field in which there are a number of methodological and definitional differences and limitations (Mello and Peters 2018: 7–8).

Regardless of the differences however, what unites the work is the growing importance of executive–legislative relations and foreign and security policy. As Raunio and Wagner (2017) have pointed out, focus has historically been on American war powers, as the main global foreign policy 'maker' (Howell and Pevehouse 2007; Dieterich et al. 2010: 8). Foreign policy has traditionally been understood to be one in which the executive dominates, with the role of legislatures stopping at the 'water's edge' (Raunio and Wagner 2017: 3). Foreign policy has also long been assumed to be less 'political' than domestic politics, as the imperatives of 'national interest' and 'national security' supposedly trump political squabbling (Raunio and Wagner 2017).

There have been several post-Cold War trends that have challenged these assumptions. If the Cold War funnelled most foreign policy decisions into one of two options, East or West, the end of the Cold War has led to somewhat of a problem in that national interest no longer seems so obvious. It is the case in Britain (and this is found on a greater scale in America) that the post-Cold War decades have been notable for an absence of clearly articulated national interests (see for example, House of Commons 2010). One consequence of this has been that post-Cold War, states such as Britain, France and other European states have regularly participated in what have been termed 'wars of choice' (Peters and Wagner 2011: 175–176; Mello and Peters 2018: 6).

Other trends have included the increasing interdependence of national and international political agendas (Raunio and Wagner 2017: 2); the democratisation of formally Warsaw Pact states (Mello and Peters 2018: 6); 'europeanisation' of intervention and defence policy (Wagner 2006). The rise of the democratic peace thesis has also been important for this body of work (Dieterich et al. 2010; Mello and Peters 2018: 11). Of significance within many democratic states has also been the issue of trust, with declining levels of public trust in governments and politics more broadly (Mello and Peters 2018; McCormack 2014) executive decisions are less easily justified. This has been a particular issue with Britain post-Cold War as will be explained in more detail in this chapter.

This particular work is a specific case study of British foreign and security policy and the relationship between the executive and the legislature. However it also contributes to the broader discussion of changing executive–legislative relations in relationship to foreign and security policy. The rapid rise and fall of Parliamentary authority as charted in the UK builds upon arguments made in one of the most recent contributions to the debate on legislative–executive relations in security, that this is a very dynamic and contextual area of politics (Mello and Peters 2018).

The rest of this introductory chapter provides a chapter break down of the work and the arguments therein.

Chapter 2

The Royal Prerogative and the Problem of Authority in an Age of Decreasing Trust

Historically in Britain, the power to declare war has been vested in the Crown. This power to authorise war is part of a broader set of powers (the extent of which is still unknown) that allowed the Crown to make executive decisions in certain policy areas without broader consultation or authorisation. Over the course of the centuries and following the changing locus of political power as Britain changed, the Royal Prerogative powers because vested in the executive (for an historical overview see Gray and Lomas 2014; Joseph 2013).

Chapter 2 begins with a discussion of British constitutional conventions, which the Royal Prerogative powers are as is the new Parliamentary convention on authorising war. The chapter then analyses the way in which the Royal Prerogative became a political concern in the post-Cold War period and the problem of legitimacy that was faced by post-Cold War British governments. The Royal Prerogative powers in general became a political issue in the 1990s and 00s because of broader political trends that became apparent with the end of the Cold War (see for example, Ministry of Justice 2007; Mills 2014). A significant discussion within Parliament and policy circles in the 1990s focused on what may be broadly understood to be a problem with a weakening relationship between the government and the people (Mair 2013). For example, a noted phenomenon in the 1990s in the UK was that of falling voter turnout and increasing delinking of core social groups from political parties (Mair 2013).

There was a sense that voters were (and are) disengaging from the public sphere. These changes are documented in a wide range of academic work looking at the shift from government to governance, voter volatility and democratisation (for example, Power Inquiry 2006; Whiteley 2011). Both Labour and Conservative parties understood that there was a significant challenge posed to government, whoever ruled, in a context in which decreasing citizen participation led to weakened authority and consequently legitimacy (Power Inquiry 2006). In response, the 1990s and 00s saw a number of legislative and constitutional initiatives that sought to reforge a relationship between the government and citizens (Radice 1996; Cabinet Office 1998; Blunkett 2001).

There were three areas of the Royal Prerogative powers that were seen to be particularly problematic in a context in which the government of the day felt that their authority rested on shaky foundations; the power to organise the civil service; to sign international treaties; and to go to war. The power of the executive to declare war without democratic authorisation of some sort was felt to be particularly untenable (House of Commons 2004).

Chapter 3

The Rise of the Parliamentary Convention on Authorising War; a Done Deal or an Uncertain Political Agreement?

This chapter charts the post-Cold War academic and policy discussion in Britain on authorising war. The British debate will be put in the context of major military interventions that Britain has been part of, as the academic and policy discussion has been reactive to major events. By 2013, when David Cameron went to Parliament to ask for authorisation to participate in military action in Syria it was widely held in Britain that a new Parliamentary convention on authorising war had been established. However, as analysts noted, there was much that remained unclear about the convention, for example, the exact scope (Mello 2017; Strong 2018).

It was the 2003 Iraq War that proved pivotal in Britain to beginning the shift away from the Royal Prerogative powers for authorising war. In the run-up to the Iraq war hundreds of thousands of people had marched in protest against American and British government plans for a military campaign and the British government's seeming support for the military campaign. In a break with the convention of the Royal Prerogative, then Prime Minister Tony Blair allowed Parliament to vote on potential British participation in the invasion, albeit on the eve on military action. Although the government won the support of the majority of MPs, the war itself proved very controversial. Moreover, that Tony Blair had constructed a false narrative of threat in order to engage in war (for an overview see the Iraq Inquiry 2016) also contributed to this debate. Following the Iraq debacle, there were a number of reports and debates addressing the need for democratic authorisation to replace executive decree when it came to war and significant military action (House of Commons 2004; Ministry of Justice 2007: 19–20).

Post-Iraq policy discussions within Labour focused on the need to get rid of the Royal Prerogative and put war powers on a statutory footing, a shift that was very much framed in terms of earlier constitutional initiatives that sought to bridge the divide between the government and citizens. However, this was a cross-party discussion and when David Cameron became Prime Minister of the Liberal-Conservative coalition government that came to power in 2009 he said that he would fulfil an earlier pledge from William Hague that Parliament would be consulted about and vote on British military action (Strong 2018). The 2011 Cabinet Manual included advice that Parliament should have the authority to embark on military operations (Cabinet Office 2011: 5.36–38) and it has been subsequently referred to as the War Powers Convention (Walpole and Karlshoej-Pedersen 2018)

Cameron sent the British military into action twice over the course of his leadership. The first time was in 2011 when Britain joined the NATO force that engaged in major military action in Libya, ultimately overthrowing Gaddafi. The action was voted on by Parliament *after* the event but the action was authorised in the first place by UN Security Council Resolution 1973 (Strong 2018). However, following on from that, Cameron went to Parliament twice to ask for authorisation to engage in military action in Syria. The first time in 2013 Cameron asked the House of Commons for authorisation to carry out air strikes against the Syrian government in response to chemical weapons use. Parliament voted against military action (McGregor and Aglionby 2013). The second was in 2015 in order to join in coalition military action against ISIS in Syria. Parliament voted in support of the action that began almost immediately following the vote (Sparrow and Perraudin 2015).

The War Powers Convention has been subject to debate, with suggestions that a War Powers Act would be preferable (for example, Gray and Lomas 2014). In 2016, the then Defence Secretary Michael Fallon said that the government would not be introducing a War Powers Act. He did however pledge that the government would maintain the Parliamentary convention and seek Parliamentary approval before deploying British forces in combat roles (Norton-Taylor 2016). It is of note however that as a convention it is not legally binding and as has been noted much remains unclear in terms of the scope and contents of the convention (Mello 2017: 82). Thus in April 2018 when May chose not to ask Parliament for authorisation of the Syria bombing she justified the decision in terms of the exemptions to the convention. However, as will be discussed in the following chapter, this decision was controversial.

Chapter 4

Syria and the Return of the Royal Prerogative?

This chapter evaluates the most recent decision by the May government to launch airstrikes against Syria without consulting Parliament. I analyse the reasons put forward by May for not consulting Parliament including the legal basis for the strikes put forward by the government. In conclusion, I argue that the justification for ignoring the new Parliamentary convention was very weak. An overview of the justifications given and the reality of the political background to the strikes suggests rather that it was exactly the kind of problematic decision-making that strengthens arguments for a War Powers Convention.

The British Prime Minister Theresa May authorised airstrikes against Syria on Friday 13 April 2018. The run-up to the bombing had been fairly short. Chemical weapons were alleged to have been used by the Syrian government against people in the besieged Damascus suburb area of Ghouta. This area had been captured and held by the radical Islamist group Jaish Al Islam, a Saudi sponsored radical Islamist group. Jaish Al Islam had been occupying the suburb for several years but in March had begun negotiations with the Syrian government to surrender in return for safe passage to other Islamist held areas. On 7 April reports were made that chemical weapons had been used. The Syrian government maintained that it had not used any chemical weapons and invited the Organisation for Prevention of Chemical Weapons to come into the area to investigate (UN 2018).

In the run-up to the strikes, Theresa May argued that there was no necessity to ask Parliament for a number of reasons that were broadly justified in terms of the exemptions to the Convention. This echoed previous statements from the British foreign secretary Boris Johnson who had also claimed that there was no need to consult Parliament. Furthermore May also argued that there was no time to consult Parliament, as Parliament would have to be recalled in order for this to happen. May did however consult her Cabinet (Rayner et al. 2018).

The decision not to recall Parliament to authorise the strikes caused controversy in the House of Commons. May explained her decision twice in Parliament, firstly in Prime Minister's Question Time and then in an emergency debate called by the leader of the opposition the following day. May set out four 'fundamental reasons' why the convention was not relevant for the action: effectiveness; protecting intelligence; the need to work closely with allies and to keep allied plans secret; that there was an existing legal basis for the intervention already, that of humanitarian emergency. May also argued that the military action the government had just taken demonstrated that putting the convention on a statutory footing would stop Britain from being able to act flexibly (HC Deb, 17 April 2018, Col 205–208).

The new Parliamentary convention on authorising war does have caveats, for example in the case of emergency (McCormack 2016). However, this is plainly intended to mean an emergency facing the country, for example an imminent attack on the territory of the state. In response to the justifications given by May for not asking Parliament for authorisation, there are a number of known matters that weaken the Prime Minister's case. Firstly, in response to the argument that secrecy and therefore surprise were of importance both in terms of the efficacy of the action and in terms of the security of British personnel, this is contradicted by reports of prior political negotiations and the week of intense publicity surrounding American decisions and White House-Pentagon debates about the scale of the strikes (Cooper et al. 2018).

Following the strikes, France announced that Russia (and by extension Syria) had been notified of where the strikes would be (Al Jazeera 2018).

Thus the context was one in which the British Parliament could not be advised about the strikes but the adversary, against whom the strikes were launched, could be. This (thankfully) served to avoid any military escalation with Russia and also meant that no civilians were hurt. The facilities that were struck had been evacuated in advance (Reuters 2018). This also meant that the strikes had very little impact. The strikes were summed up by then US Secretary of Defense General James Mattis as show strikes (Kheel 2018). Secondly, the legal basis for the strikes put forward by the government is doubtful. Humanitarian intervention does not exist as a legal framework for intervention. There is a contested doctrine called the *Responsibility to Protect* but it is of note that this was not cited by the government (ICISS 2001). Moreover, the strikes were also done in the face of a majority public opposition (YouGov 2018).

In conclusion, there seems to be little connection between the justifications given by the Prime Minister for avoiding asking Parliament to authorise the strikes and political events on the ground. Looking back at the sequence of events as documented in the media at the time, it would appear that France and Britain made a decision to launch airstrikes. America was unsure initially and France and Britain then waited until America had made a decision about participation and the level of strikes to be launched. Thus in principle, Britain could have, without Parliamentary authorisation, become involved in a far greater military operation potentially leading to conflict with Russia. With all the hallmarks of previous interventions such as Iraq and Libya based on problematic decisions taken without full democratic scrutiny, it would seem that this is exactly what the new Parliamentary convention was designed to overcome.

Chapter 5

This final chapter is in two parts. This chapter situates Britain's war powers in the context of the war powers of other European states, in particular Germany and France. The second and final part of the chapter concludes the work, considering what the position is with the Parliamentary convention on war and what is the way forward.

British War Powers in Context

This chapter examines Britain's war powers in relationship to other European states, including Denmark, France and Germany. Until the adoption of the War Powers Convention in 2011, Britain had comparatively one of the weakest systems of democratic control over war powers. As the previous chapter has shown, the development of the British War Powers convention is a very particular reaction to political shifts in Britain after the end of the Cold War.

The scope of differing Parliamentary authorities and constitutional powers in relationship to authorising war reflect differing constitutional and historical settlements. Germany and Austria for example have some of the strongest democratic war powers. This reflects not just historical experience but also constitutional divisions between central and federal units. Finland also has very strong democratic control over war powers. Any type of military deployment outside of the case of an imminent attack must be authorised by Parliament. Denmark for example also has strong Parliamentary control over war powers (Dieterich et al. 2010; Democratic Audit UK 2013). France like Britain has very weak democratic control over war powers. The French President Emmanuel Macron exercised his constitutional powers when he authorised France's Syria strikes without asking for Parliamentary authorisation. Nonetheless, the strikes were criticised in France for a number of reasons including lack of Parliamentary authorisation (Bock 2018).

However, a commonality has been a shift towards greater democratic authorisation and involvement since the end of the Cold War. The development of the War Powers Convention in Britain strengthened democratic control over war powers. However, the ease with which it was put aside suggests that in Britain this is an entirely unconsolidated shift. Despite the differing historical precedents, that other European states have strongly democratic war powers suggests that there is no reason in principle why this cannot become a consolidated political convention in Britain too.

Conclusion

Who Governs?

Britain seems to have witnessed a rapid rise and fall of a War Powers Convention. What has happened and where does it leave us? Is it the case that we see a strong executive fighting back against the new Parliamentary power? The Constitutional see-saw that has occurred over Britain's war powers must be understood in the broader context of a wider political problem of waning political legitimacy. At heart, this is a political not a constitutional or legislative problem. The latest developments in the saga of British war powers demonstrates that the Parliamentary convention is weak and easily circumvented by the government of the day. Of equal if not greater importance is Parliament's weak response despite the fact that the majority of British people were against the military action. Legislative control of the executive is at root a political matter. Legislative or constitutional controls are only as good as the willingness of the legislature to enforce them.

The question is raised about the future of the Parliamentary convention. It is both a product of and victim of broader political trends in Britain following the end of the Cold War. Weak and uncertain political authority has resulted in a political consensus that the executive no longer has the legitimacy to make decisions on its own. However, this also means that the executive must accept precisely that it does not have a free hand to make existential decisions. Recent British political history demonstrates that whether a Prime Minister accepts this or not seems to be rather a contingent decision. However, if the legislature fundamentally refuses to assert its rights and its ultimate democratic authority over the executive then there is a fundamental democratic deficit at the heart of Britain's political process.

References

Al Jazeera. (2018, April 14). *Syria's War: France Rules Out Confrontation with Russia.* https://www.aljazeera.com/news/2018/04/syria-war-france-rules-confrontation-russia-180414063828974.html.

Blick, A. (2014). Emergency Powers and the Withering of the Royal Prerogative. *The International Journal of Human Rights, 18*(2), 195–210.

Blunkett, D. (2001). *Politics and Progress: Renewing Democracy and a Civil Society.* London: Demos.

Bock, P. (2018, April 17). Macron's Bid to Look Strong on Syria Could Weaken Him in France. *The Guardian.* Available from https://www.theguardian.com/commentisfree/2018/apr/17/france-intervention-syria-macron-french-president-strikes-tony-blair-iraq.

Brazier, R. (1999). *Constitutional Reform* (2nd ed.). Oxford: Oxford University Press.

Cabinet Office. (1998). *Your Right to Know: The Government's Proposals for a Freedom of Information Act.* Available from http://www.official-documents.gov.uk/document/cm38/3818/3818.pdf.

Cabinet Office. (2011). *The Cabinet Manual*. Available from https://assets.publishing.service.gov.uk/government/uploads/system/uploads/attachment_data/file/60641/cabinet-manual.pdf.

Chalmers, M. (2013, August 30). *Parliament's Decision on Syria: Pulling Our Punches*. RUSI Analysis. https://rusi.org/commentary/parliaments-decision-syria-pulling-our-punches.

Cooper, H., Gibbons-Neff, T., & Baker, P. (2018, April 12). Mattis Tries to Put Brakes on Possible Syria Strike to 'Keep This From Escalating'. *The New York Times*. Available from https://www.nytimes.com/2018/04/12/us/politics/trump-syria-attack.html.

Democratic Audit UK. (2013). *Parliament Has Relatively Weak War Powers Compared to Legislatures in Other Democracies*. Available from http://eprints.lse.ac.uk/81420/1/democraticaudit.com-Parliament%20has%20relatively%20weak%20war%20powers%20compared%20to%20legislatures%20in%20other%20democracies.pdf.

Dieterich, S., Hummel, H., & Marschall, S. (2010). *Parliamentary War Powers: A Survey of 25 European Parliaments, Geneva Centre for the Democratic Control of Armed Forces* (Occasional Paper No. 21). Available from http://www.css.ethz.ch/en/services/digital-library/publications/publication.html/122963.

Fikfak, V., & Hooper, H. (2018). *Parliament's Secret War*. Oxford: Hart.

Financial Times. (2013). Isolationism Is Beneath Britain. https://www.ft.com/content/896db8b2-1166-11e3-a14c-00144feabdc0.

Gaskarth, J. (2016). The Fiasco of the 2013 Syria Votes: Decline and Denial in British Foreign Policy. *Journal of European Public Policy, 23*(5), 718–734.

Gray, J., & Lomas, M. (2014). *Who Takes Britain to War?* London: The History Press.

HC Deb. (2018, April 17). Vol 639, Col 192–246. Available from https://hansard.parliament.uk/commons/2018-04-17/debates/EF164C0A-E0F5-40B6-A718-DD8693A2490C/MilitaryActionOverseasParliamentaryApproval.

Hegemann, H. (2018). Toward 'Normal' Politics? Security, Parliaments and the Politicisation of Intelligence Oversight in the German Bundestag. *The British Journal of Politics and International Relations, 20*(1), 175–190.

Herbel, A. (2016). Parliamentary scrutiny of the EU's Common Foreign and Security Policy. *West European Politics, 40*(1), 161–182.

House of Commons. (2004). Public Administration Select Committee, *Taming the Royal Prerogative: Strengthening Ministerial Accountability to Parliament*. Fourth Report Session 2003–04, HC 422.

House of Commons. (2010). Public Administration Select Committee, *Who Does UK National Strategy*. First Report of Session 2010–11, HC 435.

House of Commons. (2016). Foreign Affairs Committee, *Libya: Examination of Intervention and Collapse and the UK's Future Policy Options*. Third Report of Session 2016–17, HC 119.

House of Lords. (2006). Select Committee on the Constitution, *Waging War: Parliament's Role and Responsibility*. 15th Report of Session 2005–06, HL Paper 236-I.

Howell, W., & Pevehouse, J. (2007). *While Dangers Gather: Congressional Checks on Presidential War Powers*. Princeton: Princeton University Press.

ICISS. (2001). *The Responsibility to Protect—Report of the International Commission on Intervention and State Sovereignty*. Ottawa: International Development Research Centre.

Intelligence and Security Committee. (2018). *Report on Detainee Mistreatment and Rendition*. Available from http://isc.independent.gov.uk/committee-reports/special-reports.

Iraq Inquiry. (2016). *The Report of the Iraq Inquiry*. Available from http://webarchive.nationalarchives.gov.uk/20171123123237/http://www.iraqinquiry.org.uk/.

Joseph, R. (2013). *The War Prerogative: History, Reform, and Constitutional Design*. Oxford: Oxford University Press.

Kaarbo, J. (2018). Prime Minister Leadership Style and the Role of Parliament in Security Policy. *The British Journal of Politics and International Relations, 20*(1), 35–51.

Kaarbo, J., & Kenealy, D. (2016). No, Prime Minister: Explaining the House of Commons' Vote on Intervention in Syria. *European Security, 25*(1), 28–48.

Kesgin, B., & Kaarbo, J. (2010). When and How Parliaments Influence Foreign Policy: The Case of Turkey's Iraq Decision. *International Studies Perspectives, 11*(1), 19–36.

Kheel, R. (2018, April 13). Mattis Resists Trump's Calls For Larger Syrian Strike: Report. *The Hill*. Available from http://thehill.com/policy/defense/383107-mattis-halted-two-opportunities-to-strike-syria-this-week-report.

Lagassé, P. (2017). Parliament and the War Prerogative in the United Kingdom and Canada: Explaining Variations in Institutional Change and Legislative Control. *Parliamentary Affairs, 70*(2), 280–300.

Lagasse, P., & Saideman, S. (2017). Public Critic or Secretive Monitor: Party Objectives and Legislative Oversight of the Military in Canada. *West European Politics, 40*(1), 119–138.

Mair, P. (2013). *Ruling the Void: The Hollowing of Western Democracy*. London: Verso.

McCormack, T. (2014). The British National Security Strategy: Security After Representation. *British Journal of Politics and International Relations, 17*(3), 494–511.

McCormack, T. (2016). The Emerging Parliamentary Convention on British Military Action and Warfare by Remote Control. *The RUSI Journal, 161*(2), 22–29.

McGregor, R., & Aglionby, J. (2013, August 29). Cameron Loses Commons Syria Vote. *Financial Times*. Available from https://www.ft.com/content/b16c699c-1096-11e3-b291-00144feabdc0.

Mello, P. (2017). Curbing the Royal Prerogative to Use Military Force: The British House of Commons and the Conflicts in Libya and Syria. *West European Politics, 40*(1), 80–100.

Mello, P., & Peters, D. (2018). Parliaments in Security Policy: Involvement, Politicisation, and Influence. *The British Journal of Politics and International Relations, 20*(1), 3–18.

Mills, C. (2014). *Parliamentary Approval for Deploying the Armed Forces, An Update* (Standard Note SN05908). House of Commons Library.

Ministry of Justice. (2007). *The Governance of Britain: War Powers and Treaties: Limiting Executive Powers.* Cm 7239.

Norton-Taylor, R. (2016, April 18). Ministers Drop Plans for War Powers Law. *The Guardian.* Available from https://www.theguardian.com/politics/2016/apr/18/ministers-abandon-plan-war-powers-law-mps-troops.

Payne, S. (2008). War Powers the War Prerogative and Constitutional Change. *The RUSI Journal, 153*(3), 28–35.

Peters, D., & Wagner, W. (2011). Between Military Efficiency and Democratic Legitimacy: Mapping Parliamentary War Powers in Contemporary Democracies, 1989–2004. *Parliamentary Affairs, 64*(2), 175–192.

Power Inquiry. (2006). *Power to the People: The Report of Power: An Independent Enquiry into Britain's Democracy.* York: The Power Inquiry.

Radice, G. (Ed.). (1996). *What Needs to Change.* London: HarperCollins.

Raunio, T. (2016). Refusing to Be Sidelined: The Engagement of the Finnish Eduskunta in Foreign Affairs. *Scandinavian Political Studies, 39*(4), 312–332.

Raunio, T. (2018). Parliament as an Arena for Politicisation: The Finnish Eduskunta and Crisis Management Operations. *The British Journal of Politics and International Relations, 20*(1), 158–174.

Raunio, T., & Wagner, W. (2017). Towards Parliamentarisation of Foreign and Security Policy? *West European Politics, 40*(1), 1–19.

Rayner, G., Riley-Smith, B., & Luhn, A. (2018, April 13). US-Russia 'Hotline' For Syrian Airstrikes Could Help Avoid Conflict Esclating. *The Telegraph.* https://www.telegraph.co.uk/news/2018/04/12/us-russia-hotline-syrian-air-strikes-could-help-avoid-conflict/.

Reuters. (2018, April 14). *Pro-Assad Official Says Targeted Bases Were Evacuated on Russian Warning.* Available from https://www.reuters.com/article/us-mideast-crisis-syria-assessment/pro-assad-official-says-targeted-bases-were-evacuated-on-russian-warning-idUSKBN1HL07R.

Rosén, G., & Raube, K. (2018). Influence Beyond Formal Powers: The Parliamentarisation of EU Security Policy. *The British Journal of Politics and International Relations, 20*(1), 69–83.

Schuster, J., & Maier, H. (2006). The Rift: Explaining Europe's Divergent Iraq Policies in the Run-Up of the American-Led War on Iraq. *Foreign Policy Analysis, 2*(3), 223–244.

Sparrow, A., & Perraudin, F. (2015, December 3). Cameron Wins Syria Airstrikes Vote by Majority of 174—As It Happened. *The Guardian*. Available from https://www.theguardian.com/politics/blog/live/2015/dec/02/syria-airstrikes-mps-debate-vote-cameron-action-against-isis-live.

Strong, J. (2014). Why Parliament Now Decides on War: Tracing the Growth of the Parliamentary Prerogative Through Syria, Libya an Iraq. *British Journal of Politics and International Relations, 17*(4), 1–19.

Strong, J. (2018). The War Powers of the British Parliament: What Has Been Established and What Remains Unclear. *British Journal of Politics and International Relations, 20*, 19–34.

UN. (2018, April 10). *Security Council 8228th Meeting, SC/13288*. Available from https://www.un.org/press/en/2018/sc13288.doc.htm.

Wagner, W. (2006). The Democratic Control of Military Power Europe. *Journal of European Public Policy, 13*(2), 200–216.

Wagner, W. (2018). Is There a Parliamentary Peace? Parliamentary Veto Power and Military Interventions from Kosovo to Daesh. *The British Journal of Politics and International Relations, 20*(1), 121–134.

Wagner, W., Peters, D., & Glahn, C. (2010). *Parliamentary War Powers Around the World, 1989–2004: A New Dataset* (Occasional Paper No. 22). Geneva: Centre for the Democratic Control of Armed Forces (DCAF).

Wagner, W., Herranz-Surrallés, A., Kaarbo, J., & Ostermann, F. (2017). The Party Politics of Legislative–Executive Relations in Security and Defence Policy. *West European Politics, 40*(1), 20–41.

Walpole, L., & Karlshoej-Pedersen, M. (2018). *Britain's Shadow Army: Policy Options for External Oversight of UK Special Forces*. Oxford Research Group, Remote Warfare Programme. Available from http://www.oxfordresearchgroup.org.uk/sites/default/files/Shadow%20Army%20Policy%20Report_%20PDF.pdf.

Whiteley, P. (2011). *Political Participation in Britain*. London: Palgrave.

YouGov. (2018, April 12). *By Two to One, the Public Oppose Missile Strikes on Syria*. Available from https://yougov.co.uk/news/2018/04/12/two-one-public-oppose-missile-strikes-syria/.

Ziegler, K. (2019). The Use of Military Force by the United Kingdom, the Evolution of Accountability. In *The Oxford Handbook of Comparative Foreign Relations Law*. Oxford: Oxford University Press.

CHAPTER 2

The Problem of the Royal Prerogative; Executive Authority in an Age of Decreasing Trust

Abstract This chapter provides a discussion of British constitutional conventions, which the Royal Prerogative powers are as is the new Parliamentary Convention on authorising war. The chapter then analyses the way in which the Royal Prerogative became a political concern in the post-Cold War and the problem of legitimacy that was faced by post-Cold War British governments.

Keywords Royal Prerogative · Power · Legitimacy · Government

Introduction

This chapter provides the historical and political context for the post-Cold War shift away from the Royal Prerogative powers over authorising war and the emergence of the Parliamentary convention on authorising war. The chapter begins with a discussion on constitutional conventions (which include the Royal Prerogative Powers and the new Parliamentary convention) part of the unwritten rules or guidelines that are a fundamental part of British policies. Constitutional conventions in general became the subject of political concern in the 1990s and 2000s because of a sense that post-Cold War British governments were losing authority and legitimacy. As a consequence, when New Labour came to power in 1997 the party embarked on a period of constitutional reform in response to what was widely perceived to be a problem of governance.

T. McCormack, *Britain's War Powers*,
https://doi.org/10.1007/978-3-030-13682-6_2

Although the Royal Prerogative on authorising war was adhered to for the duration of the 1990s and it would take the Iraq War to precipitate a discussion on who should authorise war; the Royal Prerogative powers in general were seen to be problematic as a form of executive action free from immediate democratic control. As Phillipson argues (2014), executive authority over war powers brings together two of the most problematic aspects of the British Constitution; the large and unspecified area of Royal Prerogative powers and the somewhat murky area of constitutional conventions, parts of the constitution that although crucial to the functioning of the British system are, in the words of the House of Lords, more of a term of art than science (discussed below).

The concluding section of the chapter examines the Iraq War and what was argued to be a significant constitutional milestone when the Prime Minister, then Tony Blair, asked Parliament to vote on British military action in Iraq.

Constitutional Conventions and Their Discontents

The British Constitution is uncodified, meaning there is no single written document that sets out the core principles and institutional relationships through which the British system functions. This is not to say by any means however that the British system is without rules or written statues. The central constitutional principle is that Parliament is sovereign and has the power to do anything but bind a future Parliament. Britain also has thousands of statutes, treaties, legal precedents and so on that regulate the powers of state institutions. A key part of the British constitution is what are called conventions.

A convention is the most intriguing thing. Conventions are a vital part of the British constitution yet conventions are without a definitive definition. Conventions may be seen as practices that govern relationships between state institutions. However, they are more than simple practices in that although if breached the party breaks no law, it would be a political problem. Dicey, as always, gives the classic definition of a convention,

> ...understandings, habits or practices which, thought they may regulate the ...conduct of several members of the sovereign power...are not in reality laws at all since they are not enforced by the courts. (Dicey 1962: 417)

The House of Lords (2013) in its report on Constitutional arrangements for Force, gives this description of what a convention is:

> In our recent report on the pre-emption of Parliament (13th Report, Session 2012–13, HL Paper 165) we considered the definition of constitutional conventions: "The word 'convention' is, in constitutional parlance, a term of art. Although there is no universally accepted definition of the term, the feature common to all definitions is that, whilst a convention is not justiciable, it is nevertheless regarded by all relevant parties as binding. Constitutional conventions may therefore be regarded as practices which are politically binding on all involved, but not legally binding." (paragraph 42, footnote 51)

Lord Wilson former Cabinet Secretary describes conventions as follows:

> I use the term "constitutional conventions" to describe the main political principles which regulate relations between the different parts of our constitution and the exercise of power but which do not have legal force. They are not themselves rules of law but many of them interlock with the law in some way. They are often as important as rules of law and can sometimes be more important, judged by the consequences which could follow from their breach. Some conventions have of course been given effect by statute and do therefore have legal force (for instance, the Parliament Acts 1911–49 which reflect the principle that in cases of conflict the Lords should ultimately yield to the Commons). Wilson (2004, 408–409)

A constitutional convention is, as Strong argues, a political rather than a legal thing. It is interpreted and reconsidered by each government (Strong 2018: 14). Conventions are not legally binding but are none the less considered politically binding. Being as the House of Lords argues a 'term of art', there is much space left for interpretation of what exactly *is* politically binding. As Marshall argues, the existence of a convention may not be disputed but its specific application in a specific situation may be (Marshall 1985: 34).

Moreover, conventions have different levels of 'political bindingness', force or embeddedness. For example, it is only a convention that the House of Commons takes primacy over the House of Lords (House of Lords, House of Commons 2006) but this is a convention that is well 'embedded'. Some conventions (thankfully) fade away as society changes, for example the convention that the Foreign Secretary should be present at royal births (BBC 1998). Other conventions may be codified, i.e. turned into legislation, by which we mean that the relationship governed hitherto by a convention may be put into written law, and therefore judiciable. An example of this is the Fixed Term Parliament Act which turned something hitherto governed by convention into a legal statute (Green 2017).

Just as with definitions of conventions, so too there is no single explanation of how conventions arise. They can be both the consolidation of practice and derived from a claim:

> Conventions are in history seen to be practices that have developed and solidified over a considerable period of time men being what they are, they tend to follow rules of their own devising; they develop habits in government as elsewhere. And when these men give place to others, the same practices tend to be followed. Capacity for invention is limited, and when an institution works well in one way it is deemed unnecessary to change it to see if it would work equally well in another. Indeed, people begin to think that the practices ought to be followed. It was always so done in the past, they say; why should it not be done so now? (Jennings cited in McHarg 2008: 857)

Jennings has this to say of the origin of conventions:

> We have to ask ourselves three questions: first, what are the precedents; secondly, did the actors in the precedents believe that they were bound by a rule; and thirdly, is there a reason for the rule? A single precedent with a good reason may by enough to establish the rule. A whole string of precedents without such a reason will be of no avail, unless it is perfectly certain that the persons concerned regarded them[selves] as bound by it. (Jennings cited in Mello 2017: 86)

As McHarg argues, conventions may be traditionally thought to develop rather than being 'made' (McHarg 2008: 857; also see Mello 2017: 86). Moreover, it is in the 'doing' that they are established (McHarg 2008: 858). Conventions then exist if we behave according to them and importantly, expect them to be enacted. An example given by McHarg is that of the Sewel Convention (McHarg 2008: 858), a principle that the Scottish Parliament must grant consent to legislation that Westminster proposes to pass that falls within the competence of the Scottish devolved Parliament. However, Munro questions the extent to which this can be seen to be a convention as such, because it was something that was instantly 'produced' rather than something that developed (also see Jaconelli 1999).

However, the Sewel convention *has* been adhered too. Elliot quotes David Lewis' classic philosophical treatise on the nature of conventions:

> Conventions are like fires: under favourable conditions, a sufficient concentration of heat spreads and perpetuates itself. The nature of the fire does not depend on the original source of heat. Matches may be our best fire starters, but that is no reason to think of fires started otherwise as any the less fires'. (cited in Elliot 2002: 361)

There is a Mobius Loop type quality to constitutional conventions in that the 'political bindingness' of a convention is the extent to which it is adhered to. However, as McHarg argues, a convention may arise from a declaration but then become a 'real' convention due to being stuck with. Conventions then are both empirical and normative, practice and intent.

During the 1990s and 2000s there was a resurgence of analysis of constitutional matters such as conventions. The British political context was a decreasing sense of governmental legitimacy and authority and this gave rise to New Labour's programme of constitutional reform (explored below also see McHarg 2008).

The Royal Prerogative Powers

The British political system as a whole has traditionally been understood to be one in which the executive has dominance. In the 1976 Richard Dimbleby Lecture Lord Hailsham famously characterised the British system as an 'elective dictatorship' (BBC undated-a). There are a number of powers found in the British constitution that are the sole preserve of the executive, of particular interest for this work are the powers historically vested in the Crown, commonly known as Royal Prerogative powers (hereafter RP) powers (Blick 2014; Payne 2008; Joseph 2013).

These powers allow the Crown to make executive decisions in certain policy areas without broader consultation or authorisation. A very significant Royal Prerogative power has been that of the power to declare war. This means that in terms of the British constitution, the Crown has historically been the legitimate sole authority for authorising measures to (in principle) protect the realm (Blick 2014: 196).

Over the course of the centuries and following the changing locus of political power as Britain changed, the RP powers somewhat travelled around. For example as Joseph has analysed in a fascinating overview, during the English Civil War it was Parliament, acting in the name of the office of the King (as opposed to the actual existing King) that exercised these functions (Joseph 2013). Following on from the Restoration the authority of the Crown and the existing Monarch were reunited. However, the authority of Parliament and Parliament's relationship with the Crown had fundamentally changed and Parliamentary powers to instigate debate and scrutinise the Crown steadily increased (Joseph 2013). Parliament itself, its form and function, also significantly changed over the course of the nineteenth century with the expansion of the franchise and the transformation of Parliament into house of elected representatives (Joseph 2013, also see for an historical overview see Gray and Lomas 2014).

Although of great importance constitutionally, the RP powers are a rather opaque part of the British political system. There is no definition of the full extent of RP Powers. Dicey gives the following often cited definition:

> ...the remaining portion of the Crown's original authority, and it is therefore...the name for the residue of discretionary power left at any moment in the hand of the Crown, whether such power be in fact exercised by the King himself or by his ministers. (cited in House of Commons 2004: 5)

In written evidence submitted to the House of Commons Public Administration Select Committee entitled *Taming the Prerogative* (2004), the Treasure Solicitors Department was frank about the impossibility of fully defining the RP:

> 2. There is no single accepted definition of the prerogative. It is sometimes defined to mean all the common law, i.e. non-statutory powers, of the Crown. An alternative definition is that the prerogative consists of those common law powers and immunities which are peculiar to the Crown and go beyond the powers of a private individual e.g. the power to declare war as opposed to the normal common law power to enter a contract.
>
> 3. Whichever definition is used there is no exhaustive list of prerogative powers. Some have fallen out of use altogether, probably forever—such as the power to press men into the Navy. It may be of more practical assistance to identify those powers which have been consistently recognised by

> the courts in the past, mindful of the encroachment into the prerogative as a result of the control exercised by Parliament and the courts. (House of Commons 2004, Written Evidence, Memorandum from the Treasury Solicitor's Department (MPP 09(a))

As Blick points out, even the most weighty constitutional texts do not provide a comprehensive list of RP powers (Blick 2014: 197). To add to this, it is not actually clear what the powers are until it gets to court (Blick 2014: note 7). Government ministers themselves have (perhaps unsurprisingly) been somewhat reluctant to identify the full range of RP powers (House of Commons 2004: 7–8). As Bartlett and Everett point out in a 2017 House of Commons library briefing paper on the Royal Prerogative in somewhat of an understatement:

> Legal and constitutional opinion on precisely what constitutes the Royal Prerogative is therefore far from clear-cut. (Bartlett and Everett 2017: 5)

The House of Commons in 2004 argued there were three main sets of prerogative powers, two belonging to the Crown and a third set that had migrated to Ministers (House of Commons 2004: paragraph 8; House of Lords 2006: paragraph 5). Thus as Blick argues, these powers might be better thought of as executive prerogative powers rather than Royal Prerogative powers (Blick 2014).

As part of an ever-changing constitution, RP powers are not something set in stone. As discussed above (Joseph 2013), those who may exercise those powers have changed as the political system has changed. Some RP powers can simply fall into misuse as they cease being relevant as society changes. For example, the House of Lords cites the power of impressment into the Navy as an example of an RP power that ceased to be relevant (House of Lords 2006: point 4). Neither in modern times does the RP allow government absolute power by any means. As Joseph (2013) has charted, RP powers may be scrutinised and challenged in Parliament via a number of ways (also see Gray and Lomas 2014). The RP can be challenged in court, as can statutory powers (see Bartlett and Everett 2017). Ultimately it is up to the court to decide if an RP power has been used correctly or has been superseded by statue (House of Lords 2006: points 4 and 7). Indeed this has been the crux of the legal challenge launched by Gina Millar against the Government's use of the RP to trigger Article 50 (Bowcott 2016).

Parliament can also limit or abolish prerogatives, it can put them on a statutory footing (House of Commons 2004: paragraphs 10, 11; House of Lords 2006: paragraph 4). Parliament can also always call for a vote of no confidence. However, despite these checks in principle on RP powers, there are serious political limitations to Parliamentary control of the executive, for example, government control of Parliamentary time table, information and so on. A vote of no confidence in the government is highly unusual as it may also directly affect each incumbent MP who provokes a general election.

The Royal Prerogative and the Problem of Governance

Having discussed the Royal Prerogative in principle, the chapter now turns to look at specific developments in Britain after the end of the Cold War that put the Royal Prerogative in the spotlight. The Royal Prerogative powers became a political issue in the 1990s and 2000s because of broader political trends that became apparent with the end of the Cold War.

A significant discussion within Parliament and policy circles in the 1990s focused on what may be broadly understood to be a problem of a weakening relationship between the government and the people (Mair 2013). There were a number of social and political trends such as falling voter turnout (discussed below) that led British political parties to feel that there were many aspects of the British political system that increasingly lacked legitimacy as political programmes and government more broadly lacked public support implicitly and explicitly. Modern liberal democratic societies have been fundamentally premised upon the idea that the state acts for and on behalf of the citizens, that the state is authorised by its citizens. As Whiteley describes:

> At the core of the modern democratic state is a relationship between the rulers and the ruled. There is essentially an 'invisible handshake' taking place in which citizens look to the state to protect and support them, and in exchange, they acknowledge they have obligations such as paying their taxes, obeying the law and getting involved in the political process. (Whiteley 2011: 10)

A noted feature of British post-Cold War politics has been the refusal of that handshake. For example, this can be noted in specific trends that accelerated in the UK after the end of the Cold War; falling voter turnout and general voter disengagement from the political mechanisms of the liberal democratic political process (Whiteley 2011; Power Inquiry 2006; Mair 2013). A concrete example of this problem can be found in the Labour 'landslide' victory of 1997 which was won with a turnout lower than that of 1992 (and this after a very unpopular Conservative government and the 'Tory sleeze' scandals of the early-mid 1990s). In 2001, the Labour Party won the election with a historically low turn out of 59% of those eligible to vote, the lowest since full universal suffrage was established in Britain (Driver and Martell 2002: 13). Political parties in Britain have also lost their core constituencies (Power Inquiry 2006).

It was not however just in terms of votes cast and increasing voter volatility that we can see a weakening relationship between the governed and the government. Another important aspect of the erosion of the relationship between citizen and state is the decline in institutions through which sections of society were connected with the political establishment, for example, for Labour the trade unions, membership of which has fallen (Moylan 2012), for Conservatives the Church of England which has also steadily lost members (Ross 2011). Linked to this has been an increasing sense of disengagement and distrust, represented in periodic crisis of the political establishment, whether 'Tory sleaze' scandals of the 1990s or MPs expenses more latterly (Hansard Society 2012) and the current scandal around Jimmy Savile and the culpability of the BBC and the NHS (Furedi 2013). Whether these trends are representative of serious political disengagement or illustrative of a shift in methods of political participation is a point of debate (Power Inquiry 2006; Whiteley 2011: 2). (The three paragraphs above draw upon discussion published in 2014.)

During the 1990s there was a very live political discussion about the need to reinvigorate democracy stemming very explicitly from a sense a decline in legitimate authority. Without that 'invisible handshake' there was a profound sense that government lacked legitimacy and thus exercised power with a weakened authority (Beetham 1991: 11). Executive government, and the Royal Prerogative, was something that seemed to be increasingly anachronistic in the face of changing British political and social values, it lacked democratic legitimacy (Blick 2014: 199).

Beginning in the early and mid-1990s areas of policy that hitherto remained opaque and governed under RP powers were illuminated by published guidelines, for example the Ministerial Code, and

Parliamentary Committees were given greater powers of scrutiny over the executive including scrutiny of treaties (Blick 2014: 200). The secret services were also subject to increased public scrutiny and oversight with the establishment of the Intelligence and Security Committee and the first ever public naming of the new head of MI5 (McCormack 2014).

The debate was most explicit within the Labour Party initially when in opposition and then when in government. There was a clear acknowledgement of a loss of traditional links between the state and citizens and the subsequent problem of governance (Giddens 2002: 7, 13; Blunkett 2001; Cabinet Office 1998: 1). Labour proposals and policy discussions focusing on renewing democracy through civic engagement, stakeholding, rights and responsibilities, transparency (for an indicative sample see Radice 1996: 7, 9, 10, 12; Giddens 1998: 65–71; Hutton 1997; Ramsay 2012: 71). The key problem that underlay all of these ideas was the need to re-engage and connect with citizens in the absence of traditional mechanisms of political representation and institutional links. On the Royal Prerogative, Jack Straw argued in 1994 '[t]he royal prerogative has no place in a modern western democracy… [The prerogative] has been used as a smoke-screen by Ministers to obfuscate the use of power for which they are insufficiently accountable' (Straw 1994).

Upon assuming power, New Labour introduced an extensive programme of constitutional change and legislation (Blick 2014: 201). A central theme running through New Labour's policy platform was that of regenerating democratic engagement in a number of ways; through openness and transparency; more local and accountable democracy: through new forms of partnership with the state; new rights and responsibilities. For example, Labour's 'flagship' act the *Freedom of Information Act* was explicitly framed as countering the serious problem of corrosion of trust in government and the need for more open and accountable government to counter that (see for example the Labour Party's 1997 manifesto); policy initiatives to regenerate deprived areas the 'New Deal for Communities' (Andrews 2004); citizenship classes in schools (Andrews 2004); 'community empowerment strategies' to increase public engagement in local government (Andrews 2004); attempts to introduce new regional assemblies in England (DTLGR 2002). A range of initiatives drawing people into partnership with government were also initiated in a number of different areas (see Newman 2005; Sterling 2005). Regional assemblies were justified in terms of reengaging citizens (DTLGR 2002: Foreword).

Overall it was an ambitious project. In terms of the constitutional literature, these changes were part of what has been understood towards a shift away from a political constitution even if these changes have been more apparent than material (McHarg 2008). Also see Elliot (2002) for discussion on the constitutional changes in the 1990s.

This programme was continued by Gordon Brown when he became Prime Minister and leader of the Labour Party. In the *Governance of Britain* Green Paper Gordon Brown argues that remaining Royal Prerogative powers, in particular the power to authorise war, are unfinished business from Labour's agenda for reinvigorating democracy. The Conservative Party then in opposition concurred with Labour's analysis of the erosion of legitimacy of the current British system. The Conservative Party's Democracy Task Force led by Kenneth Clarke began their report launched in 2007 as follows:

> There is a sense of malaise and decay surrounding British government and British democracy, reflected in widespread public cynicism, a fall in turnout and clear polling evidence of loss of faith in both the intentions and competence of politicians. It is this crisis of confidence that the Democracy Task Force was set up to address. (Democracy Task Force 2007: 1)

The report also highlighted the problem of the Royal Prerogative. The chapter now turns to consider the Royal Prerogative power to authorise war.

The Royal Prerogative and the Power to Authorise War

Although there has only been one formal declaration of war from Britain (in 1942) Britain has a remarkably consistent record of being engaged in one form of conflict or another. British armed forces have been engaged in conflict almost continuously for over a hundred years (House of Lords 2006: 5; MacAskill and Cobain 2014).

Until the 2013 Parliamentary vote on Syria there was only one substantive vote on military action, and that was at the start of the Korean War in 1950. British forces were deployed to Korea in response to a UN Council Security Resolution (Gray and Lomas 2014: 75). The Prime Minister of the day Clement Atlee allowed a substantive Parliamentary debate on Britain's actions but this occurred after the military action had begun. The motion in support of the government's then ongoing military action in Korea was carried. During the Suez intervention and the latter Falklands/Malvinas war adjournment debates were held but no votes (Gray and Lomas 2014: 76–78; also see Ministry of Justice 2007: 21 for a good overview of debates and conflicts).

For the duration of the post-WWII period this approach to authorising war seemed to fit squarely in with the Royal Prerogative powers. Moreover, this fits in as Strong points out with the traditional assumptions about policymaking in Britain, the Westminster model (Strong 2014) in which a strong executive makes policy and other state institutions support it and implement it.

The end of the Cold War was a transformatory moment in terms of conflict. Francis Fukuyama famously proclaimed the 'end of history' (Fukuyama 1992). Fukuyama was ridiculed to some extent and his argument interpreted as meaning that there would no longer be dramatic international events. However, Fukuyama as a good Hegelian meant that the era of ideological contestation was over not that 'things would stop happening'. Indeed the 1990s saw a number of conflicts in which Britain took part none of which could objectively be understood to be in direct pursuit of or defence of British interests. As has been noted in the introductory chapter, the post-Cold War era witnessed the rise of 'wars of choice' (although this is perhaps a misleading description, as there was no choice for the states on the receiving end); humanitarian interventions in which coalitions of states intervened ostensibly for the purposes of human rights and to avert oppression. It is of note too that during the 1990s (and 2000s) there was a real hiatus in great power contestation, as with the end of the Soviet Union and Yeltin's Western-backed 'shock therapy' for Russia, Russia did not engage in military posturing or conflict.

Britain participated in the first Gulf War, and military action was authorised by the executive as had been military action during the Cold War. There were a number of adjournment and substantive debates and government action was supported (for an overview see Gray and Lomas 2014: 77–84). The Labour government was elected to power in 1997 and remained in power until 2010. Labour engaged the country in several military campaigns; Operation Desert Fox in 1998, the bombing campaign in Iraq; Kosovo in 1999; Sierra Leone in 2000; and then the post-War on Terror interventions in Afghanistan and Iraq.

As Mello notes, none of these interventions were authorised by a prior vote although Parliament was informed about the commencement of operations (Mello 2017: 83). However, Operation Desert Fox and a seeming drive to war in Iraq and the 1999 Kosovo war pushed the discussion in Britain about the Royal Prerogative powers and authorising war into the public domain. In 1999, veteran Labour MP Tam Dalyell proposed a Private Members bill on giving Parliament authority over airstrikes in Iraq. It was revealed years later that this bill had been vetoed by the Queen (as is the constitutional right of the Crown, however it would seem unlikely that this veto was not directed by ministers) (Stevenson 2013; BBC 2013). Labour MP Tony Benn also raised the question of the Royal Prerogative powers in debates on Operation Desert Fox and Kosovo (Gray and Lomas 2014).

The Kosovo intervention in 1999 also precipitated a degree of debate in Britain and internationally. The intervention itself, conducted under the auspices of the 'doctrine of humanitarian intervention' did cause some controversy internationally. China and Russia used their veto to stop a UN Security Council resolution authorising any intervention. The military intervention was then conducted by NATO. In particular there were concerns about state sovereignty, potential abuse by powerful states and the right to intervene in order to stop human rights abuses (leading ultimately to the 2001 report *The Responsibility to Protect* which attempted to resolve some of these questions, see ICISS 2001).

The House of Commons Foreign Affairs Committee report found that the 1999 Kosovo intervention was illegal in terms of the UN Charter (House of Commons 2000: paragraph 128) and that the doctrine of humanitarian intervention had a tenuous basis in international law (paragraph 132). The House of Commons did conclude that the action was moral however (paragraph 138). The Kosovo crisis and the government's response to it had been the subject of several statements, day and adjournment debates (paragraph 165). However, the House of Commons Foreign Affairs Committee was also concerned about the legitimacy of the process (in particular given the absence of international legality) and recommended that in similar circumstances the government hold a substantive debate and motion albeit after the commitment of troops. The House of Commons particularly stressed the issue of democratic legitimacy, 'This will bring the United Kingdom in line with other states, and give extra democratic legitimacy to military action' (paragraph 166).

Afghanistan and Iraq

The day after the 9/11 atrocity the UN Security Council passed resolution 1368 unanimously. This UNSC resolution expressed the Security Council's full support for all necessary steps to respond to the terrorist attacks (UNSCR 1368 point 5). Britain participated in the initial invasion of Afghanistan in October 2001. There had been a number of debates since 9/11 but no vote. On the day after the military action began on 7 October 2001, Prime Minister Tony Blair announced the action to the House of Commons (HC Deb, 8 Oct 2001, Vol 372, Col 811).

As discussed in the previous chapter Britain had already engaged in military action in Iraq in Operation Desert Fox in 1998 (BBC undated-b) The Iraq issue had been rumbling on since the first Gulf War with claims of Iraqi weapons of mass destruction being a regular feature of UN Security Council Resolutions during the 1990s. Iraq had been under severe sanctions since the first Gulf War and had also agreed to regular weapons inspections by the UN. The inspections had precipitated the 1998 bombing as Iraq had repeatedly obstructed inspectors, claiming they were spying for America and Israel (something that the UN eventually acknowledged was true) (BBC undated-b). The Iraq inspections were suspended in 2005 with no weapons found (NBC News 2005).

After 9/11 there was a concerted attempt from the American government and media to connect Iraq with Al Qaeda and by implication the 9/11 atrocity (BBC 2016). For example, Judith Millar, the Pulizer Prize winning *New York Times* journalist published numerous lurid stories about Iraq's supposed WMD, mostly drawing upon information provided by Ahmen Chalebi, who was part of a CIA backed opposition group set up in Iraq, and other American government sources (Foer 2004). By January 2003, George Bush and Tony Blair were having to publically deny that they had set a timetable for an imminent war (BBC 2003a).

The political and public discussion in Britain was very different when it came to Iraq compared to Afghanistan (also see Strong 2014: 7, 8). As part of the Chilcot Report published in 2016, memos from Tony Blair to George Bush between 9/11 and early 2003 were published in which Blair explicitly told Bush to draw links between Iraq and Al Qaeda in order to gain support for overthrowing Saddam Hussein. Blair acknowledged that there was little public support in Britain and the rest of Europe for widening the war to Iraq (BBC 2016). In September 2002, what became known as the 'dodgy dossier' was published by the British government and it was claimed there that Iraq had weapons of mass destruction that could reach Britain in 45 minutes. It was later revealed that government spin doctor Alastair Campbell had personally told the author, John Scarlett, to insert these false claims about Iraqi nuclear capacity (Gilligan 2013).

As mentioned in the previous chapter, Labour MP Tam Dalyell had already attempted to pass a private members bill to give Parliament authority over airstrikes against Iraq. Labour MP Graham Allen also pursued this matter, calling for Parliament to authorise any future combat (Allen 2002). A number of debates and votes were held on the topic of Iraq in 2002 and 2003. A substantive debate and vote took place in the Commons on 25 November 2002. The debate and vote was on the motion 'That this House supports UNSCR 1441 agrees that the Government of Iraq must comply fully with all provisions of the resolution; and that, if it fails to do so, the Security Council should meet in order to consider the situation' (Gray and Lomas 2014: 20). The motion was supported by a very large majority.

As Blair had correctly acknowledged, public feeling against any war in Iraq ran high. Britain's biggest ever demonstration took place on 16 February attracting between 750,000–2 million people according to reports at the time (BBC 2003b) and polls suggested the majority of British people were not in favour of war with Iraq. Neither were major military states such as France (BBC 2003c). Within the Labour party too there were several influential MPs who were doubtful of the case for war in Iraq and over 130 MPs signed a Commons motion against any new war in Iraq (BBC 2003d).

Another debate and vote on 26 February 2003 in support of the UN Security Council resolution on Iraqi weapons was also carried by a large majority. However a significant minority, 199 MPs, had supported an amendment (which did not pass) that argued that the case for war was unproven (Gray and Lomas 2014: 39). According to Gray and Lomas this meant that almost a third of MPs had voted against war. On Tuesday 18 March 2003, as it became very clear that America was about to invade Iraq, an adjournment debate was held in the House of Commons. This was a remarkable debate. It lasted for ten hours and key government and opposition figures resigned the whip in order to vote against the government, or party line (Tempest 2003; BBC 2003e). The full debate and motion is available from HC, 18 March 2003, Vol 739, Col 760.

217 MPs voted on an amendment that argued that the case for war was not proven. In the end the government motion was supported by 412 to 149 votes (Tempest 2003).

The Iraq vote was held on the evening of the invasion and, as Mello argues, the pressure on MPs to support the imminent action was very strong (Mello 2017: 84). None the less, it was notable that the government felt the need to have the decisions that had been already made in Washington DC and London, politically legitimated. This vote has been seen as a milestone in British constitutional convention.

The following chapter analyses the political events and policy and academic discussion of the post-second Gulf War period and the seeming rise of the new Parliamentary Convention on authorising war.

References

Allen, G. (2002, September 26). A Degree of Democratic Deficit. *Daily Telegraph*. http://www.telegraph.co.uk/comment/letters/3582038/A-degree-of-democratic-deficit.html.

Andrews, R. (2004). *Theorising the Third War: Stakeholding, Active Citizenship and Democratic Renewal*. Paper Presented at the PSA Conference, Lincoln University. Available online at http://www.psa.ac.uk/24journals/pdf/5/2004/Andrews.pdf.

Bartlett, G., & Everett, M. (2017). *The Royal Prerogative, House of Commons Library* (Briefing Paper No. 03861).

BBC. (1998). *UK Politics: Talking Politics, Conventions of the Constitution*. http://news.bbc.co.uk/1/hi/uk_politics/88166.stm.

BBC. (2003a, January 15). *Inspectors Search Saddam Palace*. http://news.bbc.co.uk/1/hi/world/middle_east/2660201.stm.

BBC. (2003b, February 16). *'Million' March Against Iraq War*. http://news.bbc.co.uk/1/hi/uk/2765041.stm.

BBC. (2003c, February 21). *UK Tight-Lipped on Iraq Timescale*. http://news.bbc.co.uk/1/hi/uk_politics/2773771.stm.

BBC. (2003d, January 15). *Who's Pressing Blair Against War*. http://news.bbc.co.uk/1/hi/uk_politics/2660957.stm.

BBC. (2003e, March 19). *Blair Wins War Backing Amid Revolt*. http://news.bbc.co.uk/1/hi/uk_politics/2862325.stm.

BBC. (2013, January 15). *Royal 'Consent' to Laws Revealed After FOI Battle*. Available from https://www.bbc.co.uk/news/uk-politics-21024828.

BBC. (2016, July 6). *Chilcot Report: What Blair Said to Bush in Memos*. https://www.bbc.co.uk/news/uk-36722312.

BBC. (undated-a). *The Richard Dimbleby Lecture*. Lord Hailsham: Elective Dictatorship. https://www.bbc.co.uk/programmes/p00fr9gh.

BBC. (undated-b). *Saddam's Iraq: Key Events*. http://news.bbc.co.uk/1/shared/spl/hi/middle_east/02/iraq_events/html/desert_fox.stm.

Beetham, D. (1991). *The Legitimation of Power*. Basingstoke: Palgrave Macmillan.

Blick, A. (2014). Emergency Powers and the Withering of the Royal Prerogative. *The International Journal of Human Rights, 18*(2), 195–210.

Blunkett, D. (2001). *Politics and Progress: Renewing Democracy and a Civil Society*. London: Demos.

Bowcott, O. (2016, December 5, Monday). Royal Prerogative Takes Centre Stage as Supreme Court Brexit Case Opens. *The Guardian*. https://www.theguardian.com/politics/2016/dec/05/supreme-court-brexit-case-whose-prerogative-is-it-anyway.

Cabinet Office. (1998). *Your Right to Know: The Government's Proposals for a Freedom of Information Act*. Available from http://www.official-documents.gov.uk/document/cm38/3818/3818.pdf.

Democracy Task Force. (2007). *An End to Sofa Government, Better Working ofPrime Minister and Cabinet*. Available from http://image.guardian.co.uk/sys-files/Politics/documents/2007/03/27/DemocracyTaskForce.pdf.

Dicey, A. V. (1962). *Introduction to the Law of the Constitution* (10th ed.). London: Palgrave.

Driver, S., & Martell, L. (2002). *Blair's Britain*. Cambridge: Polity Press.

DTLGR. (2002). *Your Region, Your Choice: Revitalising the English Regions*. Norwich: Stationery Office.

Elliot, M. (2002). Parliamentary Sovereignty and the New Constitutional Order: Legislative Freedom, Political Reality and Convention. *Legal Studies, 22*(3), 340–375.

Foer, F. (2004, June 7). The Source of the Trouble. *New York Magazine*. http://nymag.com/nymag/9227/.

Fukuyama, F. (1992). *The End of History and the Last Man*. New York: The Free Press.

Furedi, F. (2013). *Moral Crusades in an Age of Mistrust, The Jimmy Saville Scandal*. Basingstoke: Palgrave Macmillan.

Giddens, A. (1998). *The Third Way: The Renewal of Social Democracy*. Cambridge: Polity Press.

Giddens, A. (2002). *Where Now for New Labour?*. Cambridge: Polity Press.

Gilligan, A. (2013, July 21). The Betrayal of Dr. David Kelly, 10 Years On. *The Daily Telegraph*. https://www.telegraph.co.uk/news/politics/10192271/The-betrayal-of-Dr-David-Kelly-10-years-on.html.

Gray, J., & Lomas, M. (2014). *Who Takes Britain to War?* London: The History Press.

Green, D. A. (2017, April 18). The Fixed Term Parliaments Act Has Failed. *Financial Times*. https://www.ft.com/content/17eda04e-ea24-359a-8c7e-d0caed79cb5e.

HC. (2003, March 18). Vol 739, Col 760.

HC Deb. (2001, October 8). Vol 372, Col 811. Available from https://publications.parliament.uk/pa/cm200102/cmhansrd/vo011008/debtext/11008-01.htm#11008-01_spmin0%20.

Hansard Society. (2012). *Audit of Political Engagement 9*. London: Hansard Society. Available online at http://www.hansardsociety.org.uk/blogs/press_releases/archive/2012/04/25/audit-of-political-engagement-9-part-one.aspx.

House of Commons. (2000). *Foreign Affairs Committee, Fourth Report*. Kosovo. Available from https://publications.parliament.uk/pa/cm199900/cmselect/cmfaff/28/2802.htm.

House of Commons. (2004). Public Administration Select Committee, *Taming the Royal Prerogative: Strengthening Ministerial Accountability to Parliament*. Fourth Report Session 2003–04, HC 422.

House of Lords. (2006). Select Committee on the Constitution, *Waging War: Parliament's Role and Responsibility*. 15th Report of Session 2005–06, HL Paper 236-I.

House of Lords. (2013). Constitution Committee, *Second Report, Constitutional Arrangements for the Use of Force*. HL Paper 46.

House of Lords, House of Commons. (2006). Joint Committee on Conventions, *Conventions of the UK Parliament*. First Report of Session 2005–06, HL Paper 265-I, HC 1212-I.

Hutton, W. (1997). An Overview of Stakeholding. In G. Kelly, D. Kelly, & A. Gamble (Eds.), *Stakeholder Capitalism* (pp. 3–9). Basingstoke: Palgrave Macmillan.

ICISS. (2001). *The Responsibility to Protect—Report of the International Commission on Intervention and State Sovereignty*. Ottawa: International Development Research Centre.

Jaconelli, J. (1999). The Nature of Constitutional Convention. *Legal Studies, 19*(1), 24–46.

Joseph, R. (2013). *The War Prerogative: History, Reform, and Constitutional Design*. Oxford: Oxford University Press.

MacAskill, E., & Cobain, I. (2014, February 11). British Forces' Century of Unbroken Warfare Set to End with Afghanistan Exit. *The Guardian*.

Mair, P. (2013). *Ruling the Void: The Hollowing of Western Democracy*. London: Verso.

Marshall, G. (1985). What Are Constitutional Conventions? *Parliamentary Affairs, 38*(1), 33–39.

McCormack, T. (2014). The British National Security Strategy: Security After Representation. *British Journal of Politics and International Relations, 17*(3), 494–511.

McHarg, A. (2008). Reforming the United Kingdom Constitution: Law, Convention, Soft Law. *The Modern Law Review, 71*(6), 853–877.

Mello, P. (2017). Curbing the Royal Prerogative to Use Military Force: The British House of Commons and the Conflicts in Libya and Syria. *West European Politics, 40*(1), 80–100.

Ministry of Justice. (2007). *The Governance of Britain: War Powers and Treaties: Limiting Executive Powers*. Cm 7239.

Moylan, J. (2012, September 7). *Union Membership Has Halved Since 1980*. BBC. Available online at http://www.bbc.co.uk/news/business-19521535.

NBC News. (2005, April 25). *CIA's Final Report: No WMD Found in Iraq*. http://www.nbcnews.com/id/7634313/ns/world_news-mideast_n_africa/t/cias-final-report-no-wmd-found-iraq/#.XBlay8acY_V.

Newman, J. (2005). Enter the Transformational Leader: Network Governance and the Micropolitics of Modernization. *Sociology, 39*(4), 717–734.

Payne, S. (2008). War Powers the War Prerogative and Constitutional Change. *The RUSI Journal, 153*(3), 28–35.

Phillipson, G. (2014). *Parliament's Role in the Use of Military Action After the Syria Vote*. Vimeo. https://vimeo.com/88916249.

Power Inquiry. (2006). *Power to the People: The Report of Power: An Independent Enquiry into Britain's Democracy*. York: The Power Inquiry.

Radice, G. (Ed.). (1996). *What Needs to Change*. London: HarperCollins.

Ramsay, P. (2012). *The Insecurity State, Vulnerable Autonomy and the Right to Security in the Criminal Law*. Oxford: Oxford University Press.

Ross, T. (2011, July 8). Church of England Faces Being Wiped Out, Report Warns. *The Daily Telegraph*. Available online at http://www.telegraph.co.uk/news/religion/8626410/Church-of-England-faces-being-wiped-out-report-warns.html.

Sterling, R. (2005). Promoting Democratic Governance Through Partnerships? In J. Newman (Ed.), *Remaking Governance: Peoples, Politics and the Public Sphere*. Bristol: The Policy Press.

Stevenson, A. (2013, January 15). *Still Powerful, Still an Accountable: Full Extent of Royal Veto Power Revealed*. http://www.politics.co.uk/news/2013/01/15/still-powerful-still-unaccountable-full-extent-of-royal-veto.

Straw, J. (1994). Abolish the Royal Prerogative. In A. Barnett (Ed.), *Power and the Throne: The Monarchy Debate* (pp. 125–129). London: Vintage.

Strong, J. (2014). Why Parliament Now Decides on War: Tracing the Growth of the Parliamentary Prerogative Through Syria, Libya an Iraq. *British Journal of Politics and International Relations, 17*(4), 1–19.

Strong, J. (2018). The War Powers of the British Parliament: What Has Been Established and What Remains Unclear. *British Journal of Politics and International Relations, 20*, 19–34.

Tempest, M. (2003, March 18). Parliament Gives Blair Go-Ahead for War. *The Guardian*. https://www.theguardian.com/politics/2003/mar/18/iraq.iraq6.
Whiteley, P. (2011). *Political Participation in Britain*. London: Palgrave.
Wilson, R. (2004). The Robustness of Conventions in a Time of Modernisation and Change. *Public Law* (Summer), 407–420.

CHAPTER 3

The Rise of the Parliamentary Convention on Authorising War; a Done Deal or an Uncertain Political Agreement?

Abstract This chapter charts the post-Cold War academic and policy discussion in Britain on authorising war. The British debate will be put in the context of major military interventions that Britain has been part of, as the academic and policy discussion has been reactive to major events. By 2013, when David Cameron went to Parliament to ask for authorisation to participate in military action in Syria it was widely held in Britain that a new Parliamentary Convention on authorising war had been established. However, as analysts noted, there was much that remained unclear about the convention, for example, the exact scope.

Keywords Parliamentary convention · Iraq · Libya · Syria

Introduction

Following chemical weapons attacks in Syria that were widely blamed on the Syrian government, David Cameron recalled the House of Parliament in August 2013 and asked it to vote on British military action against the Syrian government. The House of Parliament voted against military action (BBC 2013a). Parliament was subsequently recalled in 2015 and this time voted to join in with Coalition airstrikes against ISIS in Syria. In the aftermath of these two votes it was widely accepted in academic and policy discussions that there was a new Parliamentary

T. McCormack, *Britain's War Powers*,
https://doi.org/10.1007/978-3-030-13682-6_3

convention in existence for authorising war (Strong 2014; Mello 2017; Lagassé 2017; Gaskarth 2016; Chalmers 2013).

The Syria votes came after a decade and a half of political and constitutional debate and discussion on the Royal Prerogative powers and the specific power to decide on when to take the country to war (as will be discussed below). After the Parliamentary vote on authorising military action in Iraq in 2003, it was argued that a Parliamentary convention was in existence. Over the next decade, both parties consistently pledged that Parliament would vote on military action and indeed that there was a Parliamentary convention already in existence (as will be discussed below). Even when the government of the day did not recall Parliament to vote on military action (see below on the Libyan intervention) this was framed in terms of the convention, that the action did not fall with the remit of the convention.

For supporters of this shift, Parliamentary authorisation of a potentially existential process transforms this into a democrat and transparent process. The context for this as discussed in the previous chapter was the constitutional and legislative changes introduced by New Labour in the 1990s and 00s as part of an attempt to reforge a relationship between the government and the government. The Iraq conflict and the Labour government's role in constructing a false narrative in order to go to war also played a significant role in eroding trust in government. Royal Prerogative powers in this context are notable for their opacity and potential lack of democratic authorisation. Questions of war, peace, defence and security are particularly difficult as they are fundamentally existential questions. Underlying this, as political advocates of the constitutional shift have noted, is a need for increased *legitimacy* in such existential matters.

As Chalmers argued in 2013, the Syria vote suggests that Parliament and the public are simply no longer prepared to give the government the benefit of the doubt when it comes to war (Chalmers 2013). A YouGov report on British attitudes to defence, security and the armed forces published in autumn of 2014 also found that a majority of respondents thought that Parliamentary approval should be sought for military action of varying types, from outright declarations of war to the use of drones (YouGov 2014).

Critics and analysts have argued that there are a number of problematic implications with shifting away from the Royal Prerogative. Gray and Lomas for example argue that the convention erodes the separation of powers, that the legislature is taking on executive powers and can therefore no longer play its constitutional role of scrutiny; that it 'politicises' the decision to go to war (Gray and Lomas 2014). Another key concern is that this convention will further erode Britain's role in international affairs as a military power prepared to abide by its international military obligations (see for examples Gaskarth 2016). Here Parliament is also argued to be reflecting a public anti-interventionist stance both in relationship to specific unpopular interventions such as Iraq, but also a broader move away from support for military action in the West (Eyal 2013; Chalmers 2013). Questions of the potential for court involvement and operational quickness are also raised (see Mills 2018 for an overview).

However, despite the critiques and congratulations, it is worth pausing on the fact the convention was only adhered to twice between the period of the second Iraq War and the vote to participate in coalition airstrikes against ISIS in 2013. In 2011, the Government had refused to ask Parliament for a vote authorising military action against Libya before it had begun and the Labour party (by then in opposition) had not protested (with a few exceptions). Moreover, there are also broader questions raised about what exactly *was* established in 2013 and 2015. As Marshall argues, the existence of a convention may not be disputed but its specific application in a particular situation may be (Marshall 1985: 34). The House of Lords described constitutional conventions as a 'term of art', therefore there is much space left for interpretation of what exactly is politically binding. Conventions are political (as discussed in the previous chapter) and exist to the extent that they are followed.

As Blick argued in 2014, there are uncertainties about the circumstances in which the government of the day would be entitled to overturn the convention (Blick 2014). Mello also concluded in 2017 that significant uncertainties remained, as well as the scope of the convention, i.e. what kind of operations could be excluded (Mello 2017: also see Ziegler 2019) and a lack of specific guidelines about parliamentary procedures. These authors were prophetic as the government argued that the April 2018 military action was bombing did not fall within the remit of the convention for a number of reasons.

This chapter is structured chronologically. A chronological approach charting the political and policy-relevant debate, political developments and academic analysis has been chosen because this was and is a very live and developing issue in British politics. Policy discussion, reports and academic analysis were, and are, engaging with events and broader political trends in post-Cold War Britain and are absolutely entwined, thus a thematic analysis would I think present a slightly misleading picture for Britain. The chapter begins where the previous chapter ends and analyses the lively constitutional and political debate following on from the second Iraq war. The concluding section looks at the votes on intervention in Syria and the remaining uncertainty as to what had been established by the votes.

The Legacy of Iraq and Uncertainty Over the Existence of a Parliamentary Convention

In the first section of this chapter, we consider the intense political discussions and debates that occurred about the Royal Prerogative powers and authorising war after the Iraq invasion. Following the Iraq vote, it was claimed that Parliament's authority over war had been established. Yet these claims were belied by the ensuing political debate, in particular a number of Parliamentary Committees that investigated the RP powers and concluded that there was a need to establish Parliamentary authority over war on a firmer footing. However, by the time the Conservative-Liberal government came to power in 2010 led by David Cameron, key government figures argued that there was a Parliamentary Convention on authorising war in existence, this was also confirmed in the Cabinet Manual in 2011. Cameron engaged in military intervention in Libya and Mali but did not ask Parliament to authorise these actions. However, as Ziegler (2019: 5) argues, the government stated that a convention *did* exist but that the action did not fall within the parameters of the convention.

After the vote on the Iraq War, several key figures in the Labour government and party argued that a convention had been established that the House of Commons would authorise military action. Robin Cook, former Foreign Secretary who resigned from the Cabinet on 17 March 2003 in protest against the Government's Iraq policy, stated 'Now that the Commons has established its right to vote on the commitment of British troops to action, no future government will find it easy to take it away again' (Cook 2003: 190).

Gordon Brown also took the same view; 'Now that there has been a vote on these issues so clearly and in such controversial circumstances,

I think it is unlikely that except in the most exceptional circumstances a government would choose not to have a vote in parliament' (Tempest 2005; also Byrne and Weir 2004; Wilson 2004).

Despite these arguments, as Lagassé points out, the 2003 vote amplified calls to curb executive powers (Lagassé 2017: 285). In April 2003, the all Party group in Parliament *Parliament First* recommended that a select committee be established to review and define all RP powers and move to put these on a statutory footing (House of Lords 2004: 9). As the House of Lords Select Committee on the Constitution report *Parliament and the Legislative Process* makes clear, there was a strong sense that Parliament no longer functioned well in terms of oversight and scrutiny (House of Lords 2004: 9). Indeed the title of *Parliament First*'s report, Parliament's Last Chance is indicative.

The role that the government had played in making a false case for the Iraq war certainly played an important part in this and future debates and analysis on executive powers, exacerbating already existing concerns about legitimate government and authority in an age of diminished trust. In May 2003, controversy broke with BBC claims that the government had 'sexed up' the infamous WMD claims. These revelations (as they turned out to be) were quickly followed by the death of Dr. David Kelly (BBC 2011). The Hutton Inquiry was launched in 2003 following Dr. Kelly's death and The Iraq Inquiry (commonly known as the Chilcot Report) was launched in 2009 and finally concluded in 2016.

There were two important Parliamentary reports that followed swiftly on from Iraq; the 2004 House of Commons Public Administration Committee report on prerogative powers and the House of Lords Constitutional Committee report (see below). Three private members bills were introduced (see below). The Labour Party, now with Gordon Brown at the helm, also highlighted RP powers as 'unfinished business' from the programme of constitutional changes and devolution discussed in the previous chapter (see below).

The House of Commons Public Administration Select Committee published an excellent in-depth report on what the Committee termed 'ministerial prerogative powers' *Taming the Prerogative* (House of Commons 2004). The Committee identified several sets of prerogative powers but in particular focused on ministerial prerogative powers such as authorising the use of armed forces overseas. The Committee called a number of heavy-weight political figures to give evidence. For example, Lord Hurd argued that a convention at least should be in place that

Parliament must authorise war. Hurd suggested the possibility of legislation but worried about the question of definition of war (of which more later) and also the amount of Parliamentary time that would be taken up with legislation (House of Commons 2004).

Veteran anti-war MP Tony Benn advocated for war powers to be put on a statutory basis, as too did William Hague who advocated legislation or at least standing orders (House of Commons 2004: paragraphs 20–22). Hague was concerned that even if a convention had been established by the Iraq votes, it was not binding and would be entirely open to interpretation or just ignored by a future government in different political circumstances. Graham Allan MP and Mark Fisher also argued for some kind of statutory basis for war powers (House of Commons 2004).

The Committee made clear that the situation with the RP was 'unfinished constitutional business' (House of Commons 2004: paragraph 61) and that if ministerial accountability to Parliament was to be taken seriously, the case for reform was unanswerable (House of Commons 2004: paragraph 35). Rodney Brazier, the special advisor to the committee, suggested a bill that would require the government to supply Parliament with a list of executive powers within six months. These powers could then be considered by a special Parliamentary Committee that would then propose draft legislation on executive powers. Brazier did not concur with Hurd that there would be problems with defining what 'armed conflict' might be. Brazier argued that any bill could specify that a conflict in which international laws on the laws of war were applied would fall under the remit of a domestic war powers act, or even that that it could be left to common sense (House of Commons 2004: paragraphs 10–12).

In conclusion, the Committee recommended a 'pragmatic' solution:

> Without prejudice to its response to the Executive Powers and Civil Service Bill now before the House of Lords, the Government should initiate before the end of the current session a public consultation exercise on Ministerial prerogative powers. This should contain proposals for legislation to provide greater parliamentary control over all the executive powers enjoyed by Ministers under the royal prerogative. This exercise should also include specific proposals for ensuring full parliamentary scrutiny of the following Ministerial prerogative actions: decisions on armed conflict; the conclusion and ratification of treaties; the issue and revocation of passports. (House of Commons 2004: paragraph 60)

The government responded that it was not persuaded that placing prerogative powers on a statutory footing would improve matters (House of Lords 2006: paragraph 2). A number of private members bills were also introduced by Neil Gerrard, Clare Short, Michael Meacher and Lord Lecester (see the House of Commons Library Research paper, Taylor and Kelly 2008; BBC 2005; House of Lords 2006: paragraph 18).

In an interview with *The Telegraph* in 2005 Gordon Brown stressed that he believed that Parliamentary authority over war had been established by the Iraq vote, 'Now that there has been a vote on these issues so clearly and in such controversial circumstances, I think it is unlikely that except in the most exceptional circumstances a government would choose not to have a vote in Parliament. I think Tony Blair would join me in saying that, having put this decision to Parliament, people would expect these kinds of decisions to go before Parliament' (Sylvester and Thomson 2005). Jack Straw echoed this in 2006, and he argued to the Fabian Society that a precedent had been set for Parliament to vote on war (Brown 2006). In the same year the Conservative opposition, lead by David Cameron, launched their Democracy Task Force also pledging to examine and curtail RP powers including the power to authorise war (Jones 2006).

The *Not in Our Name* briefing paper put out by Democratic Audit, the Federal Trust, and One World Trust also argued for a war powers act (Democratic Audit et al. 2006). This paper made important arguments about MPs resources and time, and also pointed out that informal or even formal rules cannot necessarily resolve political problems. The political context is important, for example the culture or mindset of the House of Commons. Party loyalty and career prospects are also serious considerations (as indeed for most democratic states in which the legislature at least, if not the Government too, also comes from political parties).

In 2006, the House of Lords Select Committee on the Constitution released a very thorough and invaluable discussion of the RP question in a report entitled *Waging War: Parliament's Role and Responsibility* (House of Lords 2006) The Committee particularly considered the question of definitions of war, what would fall under the remit of a convention (or statute) on authorising war. As noted previously, official declarations of war have all but ceased post-WWII because the use of force as an instrument of international politics is no longer considered legitimate. Indeed the House of Lords report points out that according to the British courts Britain was not at war with Iraq owing to the absence of declaration of war; an obvious absurdity (House of Lords 2006: paragraph 10).

As the Committee observes, the British government has been engaged in a number of 'wars of choice' (House of Lords 2006: paragraphs 21–23). This is an interesting counterpoint to Rodney Brazier's argument in the 2004 House of Commons report *Taming the Prerogative*, that 'no British Government is going to take the country into armed conflict unless it is unavoidable and unless Ministers are reasonably sure that they can carry Parliament with them' (House of Commons 2004: 24–25). Certainly, in the case of Iraq the evidence is overwhelming that the government sought to go to war when it was not necessary and went so far as to make false claims to justify the war.

Two key issues that are discussed in the report are those of legitimacy and accountability. The issue of legitimacy is related to the potentially existential decision of war and the central question of who has legitimate authority in Britain to make that decision. The question of accountability is also debated. Parliament in principle can hold the government to account through debates and scrutiny. However, as a number of Committee witness pointed out, the government could control the agenda, for example through controlling information, debate time and so on (House of Lords 2006: paragraphs 42–44). Indeed as the *Not in Our Name* briefing paper argued, Parliament could be seen to have little power other than to heckle from the sidelines and after the event (Democratic Audit et al. 2006).

There were also a number of Committee witnesses who voiced concern about increasing Parliamentary involvement in the process. In summary, concerns were raised about the possible detrimental effect on operational effectiveness and coalition-working; the importance of maintaining executive authority over the decision; the difficulties Parliament might have in reaching an informed decision; the legal impact if legislation were put in place and the detrimental effect this may have on Armed Forces morale (House of Lords 2006: paragraph 48). The benefits and disadvantages of statutory provision (as opposed to a convention for example) were also discussed. Arguments in favour of putting the PR power to go to war on a statutory footing included increasing legitimacy, accountability and improving the quality of decision-making. Arguments against, included that decisions might be 'too political', i.e. swayed by public opinion (although this raises more questions about how Parliament and the government see themselves), potential for delay and potential problems with legal implications (House of Lords 2006: paragraphs 81–84). A convention by comparison was seen as more flexible. Interestingly, the House of Lords suggested that many of the witnesses the Committee interviewed already considered a convention to be in existence (House of Lords 2006).

In conclusion, the House of Lords suggested that a Parliamentary Convention would be the best way forward. The Committee noted that there was a cross-party consensus on the need to move away from the RP especially in a few key areas such as war (House of Lords 2006: paragraph 110)

1. Government should seek Parliamentary approval (for example, in the House of Commons, by the laying of a resolution) if it is proposing the deployment of British forces outside the United Kingdom into actual or potential armed conflict;
2. In seeking approval, the Government should indicate the deployment's objectives, its legal basis, likely duration and, in general terms, an estimate of its size;
3. If, for reasons of emergency and security, such prior application is impossible, the Government should provide retrospective information within 7 days of its commencement or as soon as it is feasible, at which point the process in (1) should be followed;
4. The Government, as a matter of course, should keep Parliament informed of the progress of such deployments and, if their nature or objectives alter significantly should seek a renewal of the approval.

In response to the report, the government argued that it was not yet convinced of the case for a new convention, arguing that 'it must be the Government which takes the decision' because 'that is one of the key responsibilities for which it has been elected' (House of Lords 2007: paragraph 6). The House of Lords debated the Committee Report and Lord Holme stressed that the question of the RP powers and war was at root, a question of democratic legitimacy (HL Deb, 1 May 2007).

Responding to the Committees' invitation for further comparative work on the subject of war powers, David Jenkins wrote a considered response in which he compared British and American executive war powers. Jenkins argued that fundamentally the matter of war powers was a political one. He pointed out that in America, despite Congress' constitutional powers, the President has for all practical purposes war powers not unlike the powers of the Crown in Britain. Ultimately, Jenkins points out that whatever constitutional or legal provisions exist, holding the executive to account is a question of political will (Jenkins 2007).

An Opposition Day Parliamentary debate on Parliamentary Approval of Armed Conflict was held on 15 May 2007 (HC Deb, 15 May 2007). Although it was an Opposition Day debate, the political context was, as noted by William Hague and from previous reports, one of cross-party consensus (HC Deb, 15 May 2007, Col 481). Jack Straw in response iterated that the Iraq votes *had* set a precedent and that the House of Commons was of the view that it was inconceivable that any Government would in practice depart from this precedent (HC Deb, 15 May 2007, Col 492). Straw also suggested that the government should come forward with more proposals for Parliament to consider MPs supported the proposal (BBC 2007a).

Although the government's response to the House of Commons' *Taming the Prerogative* and the House of Lords' *Waging War* was cursory, Gordon Brown, by then Labour leader and Prime Minister, did focus on RP powers. Brown hoped to reignite Labour's earlier programme of devolution and renewing government (as discussed in the previous chapter). In *The Governance of Britain* Green Paper (Brown and Straw 2007).

Brown discussed the constitutional changes that New Labour embarked on but argued there were more changes to make. Brown situated the need for constitutional change in the context of social and political changes and importantly public disengagement and the need to make the executive more accountable.

> ...(to) forge a new relationship between government and the citizen, and begin the journey towards a new constitutional settlement – a settlement that entrusts Parliament and the people with more power. (Brown and Straw 2007: 5)

One key way of doing this would be by moving prerogative powers to Parliament. As the paper states (Brown and Straw 2007: paragraph 15)

> ...it is difficult for Parliament to scrutinise and challenge government's actions. If voters do not believe that government wields its power appropriately or that it is properly accountable then public confidence in the accountability of decision-making risks being lost....

Gordon Brown made a speech in the Commons in July 2007 during which he pledged that Parliament should be empowered with a resolution on war powers:

> While constitutional change should never limit our ability to deal with emergencies and should never jeopardise the security of our forces or any necessary operational decisions, the Government will consult on a resolution to guarantee that on the grave issue of peace and war it is ultimately this House of Commons that will make the decision. I propose, in addition, to put onto a statutory footing Parliament's right to ratify new international treaties. (BBC 2007b)

What constitutes an emergency was not specified (Mills 2014: 6) and nor was it specified exactly what events the convention would cover.

A consultation paper on war powers was published by the government in October 2007. Again issues of accountability, democracy and legitimacy were highlighted at the start by Jack Straw, David Miliband and Des Brown (Ministry of Justice 2007). The paper went into a great deal of detail on issues such as the problem of definition, what information should Parliament have and whether should there be a convention or a statute for authorising war.

In the same year, the Conservative Party's Democracy Task Force published a report *An End To Sofa Government* (Democracy Task Force 2007) in which it was proposed to formalise Parliamentary approval for war. The report highlighted the problem of a lack of legitimacy more broadly in the British political system:

> There is a sense of malaise and decay surrounding British government and British democracy, reflected in widespread public cynicism, a fall in turnout and clear polling evidence of loss of faith in both the intentions and competence of politicians. It is this crisis of confidence that the Democracy Task Force was set up to address. (Democracy Task Force 2007: 1)

Following on from the consultation paper, the government published a White Paper and Draft Bill in 2008 (Ministry of Justice 2008). In the White Paper, the government advocated for a detailed House of Commons resolution setting out the processes Parliament should follow for authorising war (Ministry of Justice 2008: paragraph 215). The resolution would be relevant for Parliament to authorise the use of fore by UK forces if the use of force:

a. would be outside the United Kingdom, and
b. would be regulated by the law of armed conflict. (Annex A, p 53)

Exceptions to the resolution would be an emergency (unspecified and with the government to decide what constituted an emergency, Mills 2014: 6) and the use of special forces (Ministry of Justice 2008: Annex A, p 53 and 54). There were also a number of caveats that it would be up to the Prime Minister to make a decision about when to call the vote and rather interestingly, as will be relevant for the next chapter, that there would be no need to recall Parliament if Parliament were not sitting (Ministry of Justice 2008: paragraph 220, Annex A for the proposed bill). The full remit of the proposed resolution was not specified.

The House of Commons and House of Lords Joint Committee on the Draft Constitutional Renewal Bill (2008) felt that the proposal for a House of Commons Resolution from the government was correct. Some witnesses to the Committee however felt that the discretion that the government would allowed itself (for example, timing of a vote, judging what constitutes an emergency) would allow the government to retain so much control over the process as to undermine the democratic potential of the resolution (House of Commons, House of Lords 2008: paragraph 324). The Committee did however think that the government should commit to recalling Parliament (House of Commons, House of Lords 2008: paragraph 338).

The House of Commons Public Administration Select Committee's report on the draft bill and white paper (House of Commons 2008) was more critical in terms of its judgment of government proposals. The Committee argued that so much discretion was left in the hands of the government that there was little space for democratic oversight (House of Commons 2008: paragraphs 73, 74). As Payne argued (2008: 35) '...if you look at the options favoured by the Government, in particular the large discretionary element left in the hands of the Prime Minister, the particulars of war powers could easily end up remarkably similar to before'. Payne argued that a radical change would entail war powers begin put on a statutory footing or codified as part of a written constitution (2008: 35).

The May 2010 general election brought the Coalition government to power, a Conservative and Liberal Democrat coalition with David Cameron the Conservative Party leader as Prime Minister. As the Arab

Spring swept into Libya (Reuters 2011) so too did the British government's thoughts turn to intervention. It was clear from late 2011 February that there was a strong drive towards military action in Libya. Cameron explained to the House of Commons on February 28 that Britain expected Colonel Gaddafi's rule must end and he must leave too (HC Deb, 28 February 2011, Col 24). It is notable during that during this debate, the then leader of the Labour opposition Ed Miliband did not call for any kind of Parliamentary vote, neither did Jack Straw (as observed by Mello 2017).

It was only in answer to a question from Conservative MP Edward Leigh on 10 March that Sir George Young, the leader of the House of Commons, pledged that the government would allow a vote on military action. Of note is that Young stated that there was a convention already in existence:

> A convention has developed in the House that before troops are committed, the House should have an opportunity to debate the matter. We propose to observe that convention except when there is an emergency and such action would not be appropriate. As with the Iraq war and other events, we propose to give the House the opportunity to debate the matter before troops are committed. (HC Deb, 10 March 2011, Col 1066)

What would constitute an emergency was not specified (Mills 2014: 6) and nor was it specified exactly what events the convention would cover.

Despite this, when on 14 March Labour MP Yasmin Qureshi asked the Prime Minister if there would be a vote on any military action in Libya, the Prime Minister refereed her to the Back Bench Business Committee (HC, 14 March 2011, Col 38). It was notable as Mello has argued that despite the extensive discussion and pledges for a Parliamentary vote under the previous Labour government, Ed Miliband the Labour leader did not argue for a vote to authorise military action before it had begun (Mello 2017).

On 17 March 2011 UN Security Council Resolution 1973 was passed (UN 2011). This UNSCR pledged a no-fly zone and authorised 'all necessary measures' to protect civilians. It was supported by 10 UNSC member states with 5 abstentions (Brazil, China, Russia, Germany, India); meaning that in affect the five abstaining states were supporting the action.

France, Britain and America began bombing Libya on 19 March. A debate and vote on Britain's military action took place in the House of Commons on 21 March (HC Deb, 21 March 2011; Mello 2017: 87). David Winnick MP demanded to know why Parliament had not been recalled and the redoubtable Graham Allen (HC Deb, 21 March 2011, Col 739) demanded a more formal mechanism for insuring that the House would authorise military action in the future. Critical questions were asked abut the 'end game' of the intervention but these were to some extent moot given that the action had already begun, a state of affairs that supports Democratic Audit comment about Parliament having little power than to heckle from the sidelines.

William Hague justified the lack of a Parliamentary vote before the military action had begun because of the necessity of speed (also see Ziegler 2019: 5). However, as Mello argues, given that the push for military action had been clear and that Parliament had been discussing Libya for weeks, this was not particularly convincing (Mello 2017: 88). Hague did pledge that a further vote would be held if the nature of the mission changed and also that the government would introduce a statute for authorising war, 'We will also enshrine in law for the future the necessity of consulting Parliament on military action' (HC Deb, 21 March 2011, Col 799).

The political events in the lead up to the Libyan intervention lends support to Jenkins' arguments about the fundamentally political nature of legislative control over executive powers. The political will of the legislature to hold the executive to account is crucial. Without the will to enforce legal or constitutional rules, as Jenkins argues, the formal rules are of little account (Jenkins 2007). Given the considerable activity in the preceding years on the question of Parliament authorising war; what was acknowledged as disaster in Iraq *combined* with the known fact that the government of the day had peddled a false narrative in order to go to war, it is quite remarkable how few MPs even mentioned voting to authorise the Libyan war.

The House of Commons Political and Constitutional Reform Committee published a report entitled *Parliament's Role in Conflict Decisions* in May 2011 (House of Commons 2011a). The Committee reported that the Cabinet Secretary Sir Gus O'Donnell had written to the Committee stating that '...the government believes that it is apparent that since the events leading up to the deployments of troops in Iraq, a convention exists...' (House of Commons 2011a: paragraph 3). Committee witnesses however disagreed with O'Donnell. Professor Nigel White, Sebastian Payne and David Jenkins argued that no convention existed (House of Commons 2011a: paragraph 5, Ev 3, Q 14).

The Committee published an additional report later that year on the government's response. In this the Committee published a letter received from the Minister for Political and Constitutional Reform stating that the government was committed to observing the convention, which assumed it was in existence:

> …as the Government has already committed to observing the convention [that the House of Commons debate and vote on committing forces to armed conflict abroad], the case for urgency has not been established", and it is not therefore "appropriate to set out a fixed timetable for progress on this matter". (House of Commons 2011b)

The Committee argued however that the Government needed to honour their commitment to place the right of the House of Commons to authorise war on a statutory footing (House of Commons 2011a: 2–3).

Later in the autumn of that year, The Cabinet Manuel was published (Cabinet Office 2011). The Cabinet Manual referenced Young's statement in Parliament on 10 March and stated that the Government acknowledged that a convention had developed that Parliament would debate military action before troops were committed. The Cabinet Manual explained that the government proposed to observe that convention except in the case of emergency and if such action would not be appropriate. What constitutes an emergency was not specified (Mills 2014: 6) and nor was it specified exactly what events the convention would cover, i.e. what events would render the Convention 'inapprori-ate' (Cabinet Office 2011: 5.38).

At the start of 2013, the British government deployed military personnel to Mali. This was a response to a French request and a UN Security Council resolution in January 2013. In answer to Parliamentary questions on 31 January 2013 on the deployment, Andrew Lansley stated that the government would observe what he called the existing convention on Parliamentary authorisation of troops (apart from emergency). Lansley argued however that the Mali engagement did not involve 'combat troops' and therefore did not fall under the remit of the convention (HC, 31 Jan 2013, Col 1059). Thus as Ziegler notes, the Libyan and Malian interventions were explained under the terms of the convention rather than by denying its existence (Ziegler 2019: 5; also see Blick 2014: 205). Blick argued however that by 2013 although the RP had withered, it still endured (Blick 2014: 207).

The Votes on Syria and the Convention Established?

It was the ongoing Syrian war that was to see the convention either adhered too or brought into existence, depending upon one's perspective. David Cameron twice called upon Parliament to vote in advance on authorising military action in Syria. In the final section of this chapter, we turn to look at these political events and discussion and the accompanying academic analysis of the votes and the Parliamentary convention. In conclusion, despite the votes, there was still uncertainty about what had exactly been established.

It is beyond the remit of this work to go into detail about the Syrian conflict. Beginning in 2011 as part of the Arab Spring protests that emerged in several Arab states, anti-government protests took place in Syrian several towns. In response, the Syrian government led by Bashir Al Assad attempted to both placate some of the demands, for example lifting the state of emergency, and also responded with violence and brutality (Abouzeid 2011a). The Baathists had ruled Syria for several decades with a mix of coercion, fear and conciliation. In 2011 however it was unclear as to what the outcome of the protests would be. As reported at the time in *Foreign Policy* the protests did not reflect a broad national consensus for a number of reasons, including decades of state repression and a tightly controlled civil society, but also the relative popularity of the government and the terrifying example of post-regime change carnage in Iraq (Abouzeid 2011b).

One of the notable things about the Syrian war was that, as in Libya, the conflict became very rapidly internationalised. Saudi Arabia for example sponsored a number of radical Islamist militia groups to fight the government, including Jaish Al Islam (BBC 2018). Turkey also facilitated ISIS and Al Qaeda financially and by permitting Jihadists to cross in and out of Syria (see for example Edelman 2015), whilst Western governments sponsored many Islamist anti-government groups too. For example, the CIA engaged in it's largest foreign venture since the Taliban, Operation Timber Sycamore into which over one billion dollars went to funding armed groups, including radical Salafist Jihadi groups such as Nur Al ZInki (Mazzetti et al. 2017). As well as funding radical Islamist groups on the ground, America and other states also began a bombing campaign against ISIS in 2014. In 2015 as ISIS had taken much of Syrian territory, the Syrian government asked for Russian military support (Chappell 2015).

The Syrian war has taken a terrible toll on civilians with over 500,000 killed (Reuters 2018) and at least 5.6 million refugees (UNHCR 2018). The Syrian government has been merciless in its bombing campaign to take back areas from ISIS, as have coalition forces. Raqqa, for example, was liberated from ISIS at great civilian cost (Amnesty International 2018). Both the Syrian government (Houeix 2018) and ISIS (Schmitt 2016) have used chemical weapons over the course of the conflict.

Over the course of 2012–2013 there was intense discussion in Britain (and America) over potential military intervention and establishing no-fly zones and similar (Kaarbo and Kenealy 2016: 29–30, 39–41; also see Strong 2014; Mello 2017; Gaskarth 2016). In particular the use of chemical weapons by the Syrian government was warned to be a 'red line' (Ball 2012) for America and Britain. It is of note that America had begun covertly intervening by funding the Free Syrian Army refs and Cameron wished to do so (as reported by Al Jazeera in 2013; also see Kaarbo and Kenealy 2016; Mello 2017).

The British political context was one in which there was a serious political discussion about potential engagement in the Syrian conflict. There were two Parliamentary debates over the course of the summer, one of which was a debate on the 10th anniversary of the Iraq war (Mello 2017: 92–93) and 81 Conservative MPs signed a letter to David Cameron demanding a debate and vote in Parliament before any decision to arm the anti-government fighters (Mello 2017: 90, 91; also see Strong 2014: 13). In June 2013, William Hague notably pledged on television that in the advent of British military action, the government would ask permission from Parliament (cited in Strong, 2014: 12). A motion against arming the opposition militia groups without Parliamentary approval was also supported by 114 to 1 votes (House of Lords 2013: 9; also see Mello 2017: 92–93).

In the midst of this, the House of Lords Constitutional Committee published a report on the constitutional arrangements for the use of force in July (House of Lords 2013). The House of Lords, citing the government, found that there *was* a constitutional convention in existence but that most witnesses to the Committee were against the idea of further formalisation, i.e. a Resolution or putting it on a statutory footing. Formalising the convention would be problematic witnesses argued for a number of reasons, including the problem of definition, i.e. what kind of engagement exactly would require Parliamentary authorisation, legal issues etc. (House of Lords 2013: 51, 52).

In particular, witness to the committee raised some fundamental questions about what would constitute combat. Some witness argued that there was a clear dividing line between combat and non-combat operations with others (including Jack Straw) arguing that even arming opposition forces should fall under the Convention (see Mills 2018: 47–49 for an overview of the arguments). Concerns were also raised about the possibility of court action; potential Parliamentary involvement in operational decisions and the need to ensure political and military flexibility (paragraph 58). The House of Lords concluded that the existing constitutional convention seemed to be working well (House of Lords 2013: paragraph 62).

On 21 August, the Syrian government purportedly used Sarin gas against targets in the Saudi sponsored Jaish Al Islam held area of Ghouta (BBC 2013b). Britain, France and America pledged to punish the Syrian government through military action (France 24: 2018). On 29 August, the British government adhered to Hague's pledge and recalled Parliament from its summer recess to vote on whether to authorise airstrikes (HC Deb, 29 August 2013). The government submitted a motion that would prepare the ground for military action (Mello 2017; Strong 2014: 12; Kaarbo and Kenealy 2016 for an overview). Much to the government's surprise, Parliament voted against military action, the first defeat on military action since 1782 (Kaarbo and Kenealy 2016).

The excellent debate reflected many concerns about the action from 'mission creep' to escalating the violence and that airstrikes could not be a simple one strike but would inevitably change the UK's role in the conflict; to the lack of UN authorisation and the lack of clear objectives (HC Deb, 29 August 2013, Col 1437, see also Ed Miliband's statement HC Deb, 29 August 2013, Col 1441). As Jim Sheridan memorably stated, 'We must understand from previous conflicts that war is not some sort of hokey-cokey concept; once you're in, you're in' (HC Deb, 29 August 2013, Col 1447). Following the vote against military action the Obama administration and the French government abandoned military plans.

The reactions to the vote were intense and somewhat surprising. Rather than a celebration of democratic control over existential policy matters, a notable reaction was that the fulfilment of the Parliamentary convention was a kind of 'failure' requiring scrutiny to explain it (BBC 2014). Jonathan Eyal argued that the government had suffered a humiliating defeat and that future governments would be impeded from taking military action (Eyal 2013). As Gaskarth has charted, for many

British commentators and politicians the vote against military action was a 'fiasco' that required explanation as to why the government had not carried Parliament with it and a disaster for Britain:

> ...Defence Secretary Philip Hammond hinted it would damage the 'special relationship' with the US...The most pro- minent response was that of Lord Ashdown, a former leader of the Liberal Democrats. In a series of messages on Twitter, he stated: 'In 50 years trying to serve my country I have never felt so depressed/ashamed. Britain's answer to the Syrian horrors? None of our business!' and averred that 'We are a hugely diminished country this am'. (Gaskarth 2016; also see Strong 2014)

Fiasco, failure or democratic triumph, it was asserted that the 2013 vote had established a Parliamentary convention over war (Strong 2014: 2; Mello 2017; Lagassé 2017: 280; Gaskarth 2016). Malcolm Chalmers the Deputy Director-General of RUSI argued:

> It is now hard to see how any UK Government could undertake significant military action without the support of Parliament, or indeed of the wider public. And it is difficult to see such support being given unless there is a clear national interest involved, or if military operations are undertaken with the imprimatur of a UN Security Council (UNSC) mandate - at least until the shadows of Iraq and Afghanistan have faded much further from the national consciousness. (Chalmers 2013)

As Professor Gavin Phillipson (2013) noted in the aftermath of the Syria vote:

> It may now be said with some confidence... that, following the Syria episode, a constitutional convention exists to the effect that the Government must, before commencing any military action, permit a debate and vote in the House of Commons and abide by its result, subject to a narrow exception... where truly urgent action is required.

The House of Commons Political and Constitutional Committee however was not so sanguine in its 2013 update on the 2011 report *Parliament's Role in Conflict Decisions* (House of Commons 2013). The Committee noted that the government had failed to follow up on any pledges publish draft resolutions on formalising the convention and that the matter remained ad hoc. Following on from the Syria vote, the Committee argued that it was vital for the government to enshrine Parliamentary authority in law and that 'the de facto situation on conflict decisions appears to have outpaced the legal position' (House of Commons 2013: 5).

A number of Parliamentary Committee reports that followed on from the Syria vote also considered that Parliament's role was not quite so set as some commentators argued. The House of Commons Political and Constitutional Committee 2014 report, *Parliament's Role in Conflict Decisions: A Way Forward* (House of Commons 2014a) advocated for a Parliamentary Resolution to be agreed by the House of Commons. The proposed resolution however exempted urgency, security and special forces and also if Parliament were dissolved at the time. The Committee's report on the Role and Powers of the Prime Minister (House of Commons 2014b) also recommended clarifying and formalising remaining RP powers such as the that of going to war (16) also see the Committees report on *Revisiting the Cabinet Manuel* (House of Commons 2015).

In September 2014, Cameron made several statements to the House of Commons confirming that there was a Parliamentary Convention for authorisation of war in the case of premeditated military action but excluded situations of emergency or humanitarian crisis (Mills 2018: 31). Cameron argued that the Parliamentary Convention applied to cases of premeditated military action and he also clarified what did not fall under the remit of the Convention, for example action in defence of critical national interests or humanitarian emergency:

> ... Let me be clear: I think the convention that has grown up in recent years that the House of Commons is properly consulted and there is a proper vote is a good convention. It is particularly apt when there is—as there is today—a proposal for, as it were, premeditated military action. I think it is important to reserve the right that if there were a critical British national interest at stake or there were the need to act to prevent a humanitarian catastrophe, you could act immediately and explain to the House of Commons afterwards. I am being very frank about this because I do not want to mislead anybody. (HC, 26 September 2014, Col 1265)

Cameron also used drone strikes to execute two British citizens fighting with ISIS in Syria in August (Wintour and Watt 2015), he did not ask Parliament for authorisation but justified this in terms of the convention.

The British government argued that it had been acting in an emergency situation and therefore the action did not fall under the remit of the convention (see Strong 2018: 27 for details; also McCormack 2016).

In December 2015, Cameron again went to the House of Commons to ask for authorisation to engage in military action in Syria. This time however Cameron asked for authorisation to join in with the military coalition conducting airstrikes against ISIS in Syria. MPs voted in favour of the action by 397 to 223 (Sparrow and Perraudin 2015).

The following year the then Defence Secretary Michal Fallon clarified to the House of Commons what would fall under the remit of the Parliamentary Convention. Fallon stated that the deployment of a military training team to Ukraine was not an 'offensive military operation' and therefore outside of the remit of the Parliamentary Convention:

> There is a well established convention that if we are engaged in offensive military operations in a country we would of course come to the House [...] This [the Ukraine deployment], however, is not a military operation. We are providing trainers and advisers to help the armed forces of Ukraine better to defend themselves and to help reduce the very high number of fatalities and casualties that they are suffering. (Fallon cited in Mills 2018: 35)

The government however also decided against formalising the convention by putting it on a statutory basis. Fallon explained in a written statement that the government acknowledged and observed the Convention and explained the exceptions to the Convention and why the Government did not wish to formalise the Convention further:

> The Cabinet Manual states, "In 2011, the Government acknowledged that a Convention had developed in Parliament that before troops were committed the House of Commons should have an opportunity to debate the matter and said that it proposed to observe that Convention except where there was an emergency and such action would not be appropriate".
>
> The Prime Minister repeated this commitment in relation to Libya in Parliament on 16 March 2016. The Convention relates to conflict decisions rather than routine deployments of the UK Armed Forces around the world. The exception to the Convention is important to ensure that this and future Governments can use their judgement about how best to protect the security and interests of the UK.
>
> In observing the Convention, we must ensure that the ability of our Armed Forces to act quickly and decisively, and to maintain the security of

> their operations, is not compromised. The Prime Minister, the Attorney General and I have set out the Government's interpretation of the Convention on a number of occasions.
>
> After careful consideration, the Government has decided that it will not be codifying the Convention in law or by resolution of the House in order to retain the ability of this and future Governments and the Armed Forces to protect the security and interests of the UK in circumstances that we cannot predict, and to avoid such decisions becoming subject to legal action. (HC, Written Statement, 18 April 2016)

Revelations that year of British special forces training Western-backed anti-Syrian government militias (BBC 2016) passed, as Strong points out, without notice in Parliament (Strong 2018: 27).

What Was Established by the Syria Votes?

Cameron's decisions to recall Parliament to authorise air strikes against the Syrian government in 2013 and then against ISIS in Syria in 2015 were heralded as a significant moment of constitutional change, for good or for ill. Whilst the Defence Secretary made clear that the government would not be formalising the convention by putting it on a statutory basis or passing a resolution, key figures in the government repeatedly argued that there was a convention in existence and that the government would adhere to it.

But what exactly was established by the Convention? It seems to be that what had been established is that Parliament would be asked to give prior approval in the case of premeditated military action probably involving troops in an offensive role. Retrospective approval would be asked for if the operation was/is a non-combat one or the action was/is required to protect a critical national interest or to prevent an imminent humanitarian catastrophe (Ziegler 2019; Mills 2018: 35; Fallon above, HC Written Statement, 18 April 2016). Cases of emergency and also of use of what Rogers has termed remote control war for example special forces, drones (HC Written Statement, 18 April 2016; McCormack 2016) are not considered to be within the remit of the Convention.

Moreover, it rests with the government to decide on what constitutes emergency, or indeed national interests (see Mills 2018: 50–51 for a description of how the Ministry of Defence defines national interests). Matters of timing and also of information are also still within the remit of the government, yet these are two matters that, regardless of convention or more formal rules, give government the upper hand over Parliament (see also Democratic Audit et al. 2008). Furthermore, the Convention allows the government to define a number of key issues; for example, what constitutes a combat or offensive role. As discussed above, this question of definition of conflict has been one that has been a significant part of the debate (see Mills 2018: 47–49). Fallon, in his written answer of 2016 above, left the government an extremely wide remit when he stated that it was up to the government to decide if the situation was 'appropriate'. A suggestion that the government will adhere to the convention, apart from when it does not wish to.

Cameron did however adhere to the convention. It is of note that the 2013 vote on the Syria strikes was about *air strikes*, there was no suggestion that Britain was going to send in ground troops. In principle then in terms of the remit of the convention, Cameron could have simply engaged in air strikes (as Theresa May did in April 2018) and justified not asking for Parliamentary authorisation because it did not fall under the remit of the Convention. Cameron's decision can be explained by the political context in the run-up to the vote, for example debates, letters from MPs warning against arming the anti-government militias (see above and also Mello 2017: 92–93). An important part of this debate in the run-up to the vote, and in the House of Commons debate and vote, was on the question of the impact of strikes, to return to Jim Sheridan pithy summary about war not being some sort of hokey-cokey concept; once you're in, you're in. In reality, the line between offensive military operations and other types of military operations is not clear cut.

None the less, the remit of the convention is not specified. As Blick argued in 2014, whilst it might be generally agreed that there is some kind of war powers convention, what is not agreed is a precise definition of when exactly the convention will apply (Blick 2014: 195). As Mello concluded in 2017,

> although the notion of a new convention is widely shared among political actors, its *scope* and *contents* remain contested. Specifically, there is disagreement about (1) the kind of operations that ought to be exempt from the rule that parliament should be asked before military deployments, (2) questions of parliamentary procedure that favour the executive and, crucially, (3) the proper timing of substantive votes before the initiation of military operations. (Mello 2017: 82; also see Strong 2018)

This ambiguity can be understood in the broader context of constitutional conventions more broadly. As discussed in Chapter 1, the existence of a convention may be widely accepted but its application in a specific situation may not be accepted (Marshall 1985: 34). Moreover, the essentially 'political' nature of the convention means that they exist to the extent that they are followed. Although, as Kaarbo has pointed out, even legislation on war powers does not prevent disagreements about the exact scope and application (Kaarbo 2018: 38). This is supported by the consideration of American war powers, as David Jenkins illustrated (2007). Constraints (whether constitutional or statutory) are only as good as the political will that underpins them. In this particular case, where the government in essence stated that it would follow the convention apart from when it did not wish to, the convention seems to be even looser than would normally be understood.

The following chapter analyses the events of April 2018 and the government's bombing of Syria. The Parliamentary Convention was not adhered to by Theresa May, however the Convention was negatively acknowledged (Ziegler 2019) as the government argued that the action fell outside of the remit of the Convention. Charting the events of April 2018 in the run-up to the bombing, it will be argued that the government's justifications for not adhering to the convention do not stand up to scrutiny. Certainly the situation was little different, and markedly more perilous in terms of potential military escalation, than when Cameron recalled Parliament to authorise strikes against the Syrian government in 2013. Moreover, as will be discussed, the government also sought to narrow the convention so as to justify its arguments.

This then supports analysis above that whilst there might be general acceptance of the existence of a Convention, the scope and contents remain undefined, in effect leaving the Convention to the mercy of the government of the day and arguably therefore irrelevant.

References

Abouzeid, R. (2011a, March 24). With Syria on the Brink Assad Promises Reform. *Time*. Available from http://content.time.com/time/world/article/0,8599,2061288,00.html.

Abouzeid, R. (2011b, March 6). Sitting Pretty in Syria: Why Few Go Bashing Bashar. *Time*. Available from http://content.time.com/time/world/article/0,8599,2057067-2,00.html.

Al Jazeera. (2013, November 18). *Obama Signs Secret Order to Aid Syria Rebels.* https://www.aljazeera.com/news/middleeast/2012/08/20128264510724249.html.

Amnesty International. (2018). *Syria: US-Led Coalition's Aerial Attacks in Raqqa Killed Hundreds of Civilians.* Available from https://www.amnesty.org.uk/press-releases/syria-us-led-coalitions-aerial-attacks-raqqa-killed-hundreds-civilians-new-report.

Ball, J. (2012, August 20). Obama Issues Syria a 'Red Line' Warning on Chemical Weapons. *The Washington Post.* https://www.washingtonpost.com/world/national-security/obama-issues-syria-red-line-warning-on-chemical-weapons/2012/08/20/ba5d26ec-eaf7-11e1-b811-09036bcb182b_story.html?noredirect=on&utm_term=.4fd4eeabacc8.

BBC. (2005, May 27). *Short in Mandatory War Vote Bid.* http://news.bbc.co.uk/1/hi/uk_politics/4585777.stm.

BBC. (2007a, May 15). *MPs Support War-Powers Proposals.* http://news.bbc.co.uk/1/hi/uk_politics/6658161.stm.

BBC. (2007b, July 3). *In Full: Brown on Constitution.* http://news.bbc.co.uk/1/hi/uk_politics/6266526.stm.

BBC. (2011, December 17). *Dr. David Kelly: Controversial Death Examined.* https://www.bbc.co.uk/news/uk-13716127.

BBC. (2013a). https://www.bbc.co.uk/news/uk-21009663.

BBC. (2013b, September 24). *Syria Chemical Attack: What We Know.* https://www.bbc.co.uk/news/world-middle-east-23927399.

BBC. (2014, November 10). *Shaun Ley, How Did the Government Let a Defeat Over Syria Happen.* https://www.bbc.co.uk/news/uk-politics-29985110.

BBC. (2016, August 8). *Quentin Sommerville, UK Special Forces Pictured on the Ground in Syria.* https://www.bbc.co.uk/news/uk-37015915.

BBC. (2018). *House of Saud, Producer Michael Radford.* Available from https://www.bbc.co.uk/programmes/b09m53py.

Blick, A. (2014). Emergency Powers and the Withering of the Royal Prerogative. *The International Journal of Human Rights, 18*(2), 195–210.

Brown, C. (2006, June 28). Straw to Call for End to Prime Minister's Royal Prerogative on War. *The Independent.* https://www.independent.co.uk/news/uk/politics/straw-to-call-for-end-to-prime-ministers-royal-prerogative-on-war-6096954.html.

Brown, G., & Straw, J. (2007). *The Governance of Britain, Green Paper.* https://assets.publishing.service.gov.uk/government/uploads/system/uploads/attachment_data/file/228834/7170.pdf.

Byrne, I., & Weir, S. (2004). Democratic Audit: Executive Democracy in War and Peace. *Parliamentary Affairs, 57*(2), 453–468.

Cabinet Office. (2011). *The Cabinet Manual.* Available from https://assets.publishing.service.gov.uk/government/uploads/system/uploads/attachment_data/file/60641/cabinet-manual.pdf.

Chalmers, M. (2013, August 30). *Parliament's Decision on Syria: Pulling Our Punches.* RUSI Analysis. https://rusi.org/commentary/parliaments-decision-syria-pulling-our-punches.

Chappell, B. (2015, September 30). *Russia Begins Airstrikes in Syria After Assad's Request.* National Public Radio. Available from https://www.npr.org/sections/thetwo-way/2015/09/30/444679327/russia-begins-conducting-airstrikes-in-syria-at-assads-request.

Cook, R. (2003). *The Point of Departure.* New York, NY: Simon & Schuster.

Democracy Task Force. (2007). *An End to Sofa Government, Better Working of Prime Minister and Cabinet.* Available from http://image.guardian.co.uk/sys-files/Politics/documents/2007/03/27/DemocracyTaskForce.pdf.

Democratic Audit, The Federal Trust, & One World Trust. (2006). *Not in Our Name.*

Democratic Audit, The Federal Trust, & One World Trust. (2008). *A World of Difference.*

Edelman, E. S. (2015, August 27). America's Dangerous Bargain With Turkey. *The New York Times.* Available from https://www.nytimes.com/2015/08/27/opinion/americas-dangerous-bargain-with-turkey.html?_r=1.

Eyal, J. (2013). *Voting for Irrelevance? The UK Parliament Passes Its Verdict.* RUSI Newsbrief. Available from https://www.rusi.org/go.php?structureID=articles_newsbrief&ref=A5225CB57962BB#.VWWhpEuvvFI.

France 24. (2018, April 14). *A History of the Syria Chemical Weapons 'Red Line'.* https://www.france24.com/en/20180414-syria-chemical-weapons-red-line-obama-macron-assad-russia-usa-france-idlib.

Gaskarth, J. (2016). The Fiasco of the 2013 Syria Votes: Decline and Denial in British Foreign Policy. *Journal of European Public Policy, 23*(5), 718–734.

Gray, J., & Lomas, M. (2014). *Who Takes Britain to War?* London: The History Press.

HC. (2011, March 14). Vol 525, Col 38. Available from https://publications.parliament.uk/pa/cm201011/cmhansrd/cm110314/debtext/110314-0001.htm#11031411000731.

HC. (2013, January 31). Vol 557, Col 1059. Available from https://publications.parliament.uk/pa/cm201213/cmhansrd/cm130131/debtext/130131-0001.htm#13013128000706.

HC. (2014, September 26). Vol 585, Col 1265. Available from https://publications.parliament.uk/pa/cm201415/cmhansrd/cm140926/debtext/140926-0001.htm.

HC Deb. (2007, May 15). Vol 460, Col 481. Available from https://publications.parliament.uk/pa/cm200607/cmhansrd/cm070515/debindx/70515-x.htm.

HC Deb. (2011, February 28). Vol 524, Col 24. Available from https://publications.parliament.uk/pa/cm201011/cmhansrd/cm110228/debtext/110228-0001.htm#11022819000002.

HC Deb. (2011, March 10). Vol 524, Col 1066. Available from https://publications.parliament.uk/pa/cm201011/cmhansrd/cm110310/debtext/110310-0001.htm.

HC Deb. (2011, March 21). Vol 527, Col 700–801. Available from https://publications.parliament.uk/pa/cm201011/cmhansrd/cm110321/debtext/110321-0002.htm.

HC Deb. (2013, August 29). Vol 566, Col 1425. Available from https://publications.parliament.uk/pa/cm201314/cmhansrd/cm130829/debtext/130829-0001.htm.

HC Written Statement. (2016, April 18). HCWS678. Available from https://www.parliament.uk/written-questions-answers-statements/written-statement/Commons/2016-04-18/HCWS678.

HL Deb. (2007, May 1). Vol 691, Col 979. Available from https://publications.parliament.uk/pa/ld200607/ldhansrd/index/070501.html#contents.

Houeix, R. (2018, April 16). *A History of the Syria Chemical Weapons 'Red Line'*. France 24. Available from http://www.france24.com/en/20180414-syria-chemical-weapons-red-line-obama-macron-assad-russia-usa-france-idlib.

House of Commons. (2004). Public Administration Select Committee, *Taming the Royal Prerogative: Strengthening Ministerial Accountability to Parliament*. Fourth Report Session 2003–04, HC 422.

House of Commons. (2008). Public Administration Select Committee First Report, *Constitutional Renewal: Draft Bill and White Paper*. Tenth Report of Session 2007–08, HC 499.

House of Commons. (2011a). Political and Constitutional Reform Committee, *Parliament's Role in Conflict Decisions*. Eight Report of Session 2010–12, HC 923.

House of Commons. (2011b). Political and Constitutional Reform Committee, *Parliament's Role in Conflict Decisions, Further Government Response*. Twelfth Report of Session 2010–12, HC 1673.

House of Commons. (2013). Political and Constitutional Reform Committee, *Parliament's Role in Conflict Decisions: An Update*. Eight Report of Session 2013–14.

House of Commons. (2014a). Political and Constitutional Reform Committee, *Parliament's Role in Conflict Decisions: A Way Forward*. Twelfth Report of Session 2013–14, HC 892.

House of Commons. (2014b). Political and Constitutional Reform Committee, *Role and Powers of the Prime Minister*. First Report of Session 2014–15, HC 351.

House of Commons. (2015). Political and Constitutional Reform Committee, *Revisiting the Cabinet Manual*. Fifth Report of Session 2014–15.

House of Lords. (2004). Select Committee on the Constitution, *Parliament and the Legislative Process*. 14th Report of Session 2003–4, HL Paper 173-I.

House of Lords. (2006). Select Committee on the Constitution, *Waging War: Parliament's Role and Responsibility*. 15th Report of Session 2005–06, HL Paper 236-I.

House of Lords. (2007). Select Committee on the Constitution, *Waging War: Parliament's Role and Responsibility, Follow Up*. Report 15th Report of Session 2006–07, HL Paper 51.

House of Lords. (2013). Constitution Committee, Second Report, *Constitutional Arrangements for the Use of Force*. HL Paper 46.

House of Lords, House of Commons (2008). Joint Committee on the Draft Constitutional Renewal Bill, Session 2007–08, HL Paper 166-I HC Paper 551-I.

Jenkins, D. (2007). Constitutional Reform Goes to War: Some Lessons from the United States. *Public Law*, 258–279.

Jones, G. (2006, February 6). Cameron Seeks to Limit Blair's Use of Royal Prerogative. *The Daily Telegraph*. https://www.telegraph.co.uk/news/uknews/1509778/Cameron-seeks-to-limit-Blairs-use-of-Royal-Prerogative.html.

Kaarbo, J. (2018). Prime Minister Leadership Style and the Role of Parliament in Security Policy. *The British Journal of Politics and International Relations, 20*(1), 35–51.

Kaarbo, J., & Kenealy, D. (2016). No, Prime Minister: Explaining the House of Commons' Vote on Intervention in Syria. *European Security, 25*(1), 28–48.

Lagassé, P. (2017). Parliament and the War Prerogative in the United Kingdom and Canada: Explaining Variations in Institutional Change and Legislative Control. *Parliamentary Affairs, 70*(2), 280–300.

Marshall, G. (1985). What Are Constitutional Conventions? *Parliamentary Affairs, 38*(1), 33–39.

Mazzetti, M., Goldman, A., & Schmidt, M. (2017, August 2). Behind the Sudden Death of a $1 Billion Secret CIA War in Syria. *The New York Times*. https://www.nytimes.com/2017/08/02/world/middleeast/cia-syria-rebel-arm-train-trump.html.

McCormack, T. (2016). The Emerging Parliamentary Convention on British Military Action and Warfare by Remote Control. *The RUSI Journal, 161*(2), 22–29.

Mello, P. (2017). Curbing the Royal Prerogative to Use Military Force: The British House of Commons and the Conflicts in Libya and Syria. *West European Politics, 40*(1), 80–100.

Mills, C. (2014). *Parliamentary Approval for Deploying the Armed Forces, An Update* (Standard Note SN05908). House of Commons Library.

Mills, C. (2018). *Parliamentary Approval for Military Action* (Commons Briefing Paper 7166). House of Commons Library.

Ministry of Justice. (2007). *The Governance of Britain: War Powers and Treaties: Limiting Executive Powers*. Cm 7239.

Ministry of Justice. (2008). *The Governance of Britain: Constitutional Renewal*. Cm 7342-I.

Payne, S. (2008). War Powers the War Prerogative and Constitutional Change. *The RUSI Journal, 153*(3), 28–35.

Phillipson, G. (2013, September 19). *'Historic' Commons' Syria Vote: The Constitutional Significance (Part I)*. UK Const. L. Blog. Available at http://ukconstitutionallaw.org.

Reuters. (2011, August 22). *Timeline: Libya's Uprising Against Muammar Gaddafi*. https://www.reuters.com/article/us-libya-events-idUSTRE77K2QH20110822.

Reuters. (2018, March 12). *Syrian Observatory Says War Has Killed More Than Half a Million*. Available from https://www.reuters.com/article/us-mid-east-crisis-syria/syrian-observatory-says-war-has-killed-more-than-half-a-million-idUSKCN1GO13M.

Schmitt, E. (2016, November 21). *ISIS Used Chemical Arms at Least 52 Times in Syria and Iraq, Report Says*. https://www.nytimes.com/2016/11/21/world/middleeast/isis-chemical-weapons-syria-iraq-mosul.html.

Sparrow, A., & Perraudin, F. (2015, December 3). Cameron Wins Syria Airstrikes Vote by Majority of 174—As It Happened. *The Guardian*. Aavailable from https://www.theguardian.com/politics/blog/live/2015/dec/02/syria-airstrikes-mps-debate-vote-cameron-action-against-isis-live.

Strong, J. (2014). Why Parliament Now Decides on War: Tracing the Growth of the Parliamentary Prerogative Through Syria, Libya and Iraq. *British Journal of Politics and International Relations, 17*(4), 1–19.

Strong, J. (2018). The War Powers of the British Parliament: What Has Been Established and What Remains Unclear. *British Journal of Politics and International Relations, 20*, 19–34.

Sylvester, R., & Thomson, A. (2005, April 30). Brown: I Would Give MPs Last Word on War. *The Daily Telegraph*. https://www.telegraph.co.uk/news/uknews/1488989/Brown-I-would-give-MPs-last-word-on-war.html.

Taylor, C., & Kelly, R. (2008). *Parliamentary Approval for Deploying the Armed Forces: An Introduction to the Issues* (Research Paper 08/08). House of Commons Library.

Tempest, M. (2005, August 11). *Inquiry to Look at MPs' Role in Declaring War*. https://www.theguardian.com/politics/2005/aug/11/houseofcommons.

UN. (2011, March 17). *Security Council 6498th Meeting, SC/10200*. https://www.un.org/press/en/2011/sc10200.doc.htm.

UNHCR. (2018). *Syria Emergency*. Available from http://www.unhcr.org/uk/syria-emergency.html.

Wilson, R. (2004). The Robustness of Conventions in a Time of Modernisation and Change. *Public Law* (Summer), 407–420.

Wintour, P., & Watt, N. (2015, September 7). UK Forces Kill British Isis Fighters in Targeted Drone Strike on Syrian City. *The Guardian*. https://www.theguardian.com/uk-news/2015/sep/07/uk-forces-airstrike-killed-isis-briton-reyaad-khan-syria.

Yougov. (2014). *Report on British Attitudes to Defence, Security and the Armed Forces, Survey Results Pages 6–10*. Available from http://cdn.yougov.com/cumulus_uploads/document/uv4r28gl4x/B_DEFSEC_2.pdf.

Ziegler, K. (2019). The Use of Military Force by the United Kingdom, the Evolution of Accountability. In *The Oxford Handbook of Comparative Foreign Relations Law*. Oxford: Oxford University Press.

CHAPTER 4

Syria and the Return of the Royal Prerogative?

Abstract This chapter evaluates the most recent decision by the May government to launch airstrikes against Syria without consulting Parliament. I analyse the reasons put forward by May for not consulting Parliament including the legal basis for the strikes put forward by the government. In conclusion, I argue that the justification for ignoring the new Parliamentary Convention was very weak. An overview of the justifications given and the reality of the political background to the strikes suggests rather that it was exactly the kind of problematic decision-making that strengthens arguments for a War Powers Convention.

Keywords Theresa May · Syria · Bombing · Trump · France

Introduction

This chapter analyses the most recent decision by the Conservative government led by Prime Minister Theresa May to launch airstrikes against Syria without asking Parliament for authorisation. Prime Minister Theresa May acknowledged the existence of the convention and explained to the House of Commons that there were four 'fundamental reasons' why the convention was not relevant for the action: effectiveness; protecting intelligence; the need to work closely with allies and to keep allied plans secret; that there was an existing legal basis for the intervention already, that of humanitarian emergency. May also argued

T. McCormack, *Britain's War Powers*,
https://doi.org/10.1007/978-3-030-13682-6_4

that the military action the government had just taken demonstrated that putting the Convention on a statutory footing would stop Britain from being able to act flexibly (HC Deb, 17 April 2018, Col 205–208). Discussed in more detail below.

In this chapter it will be argued that the justifications given by the British Prime Minister to launch airstrikes without consulting Parliament are, to put it charitably, not very strong. Firstly, the justifications given by May are not supported by known facts. For example, far from the strikes being a secret, there had been several days discussion with Russia (and by extension the Syrian government would have been informed of the strikes) in order to stop military escalation between Russia and America, France and Britain. The legal basis for the strikes put forward by the government is also doubtful, at best the grounds of humanitarian intervention are contested. Finally, the strikes were done with little public support. In conclusion, I will argue that the Parliamentary convention was ignored for unpersuasive reasons. Rather, a consideration of the arguments suggests that it is precisely this sort of problematic decision-making that has led to the Parliamentary convention on authorising war in the first place.

Moreover, Cameron had asked Parliament to authorise *airstrikes* in 2013 (and in 2015), despite the convention generally being assumed to be relevant for planned large scale offensive military action. May authorised the kind of operation that was exactly like that proposed by Cameron in 2013. As discussed in the previous chapter, significant questions had been raised about whether one could divide military action and engagement in a conflict neatly and simply dip in and out as one chose without escalation or being drawn in. In the case of the April 2018 airstrikes, Russia had explicitly warned that if Russian military personnel were harmed Russia would retaliate (see below for references). Thus the states in April 2018 were considerably higher not only for Britain but potentially globally than in 2013.

The ease with which the government could justify avoiding the convention *and* that there was little political pressure on the government either in the run-up to the strikes or afterwards confirms analysis after the 2013 Syria vote that the Convention remains uncertain. Key questions about scope and definitions remain. As analysis of conventions had shown (Chapter 2), conventions are fundamentally political parts of the constitution and depend ultimately on political will. In conclusion, it is the House of Commons that has abdicated its political role of holding the executive to account.

Moreover, in the case of this particular convention even the looseness traditionally associated with conventions does not do justice to the wide remit that the government has left itself. As Fallon explained in 2016, the Government 'proposed to observe that Convention except where there was an emergency and such action would not be appropriate' (HC Written Statement, 18 April 2016). That is to say, the government proposed to observe the convention when it chose to but not when it thought it ought not.

Run-Up to the Strikes

Parliament's vote against airstrikes in 2013 resulted in America and France also not carrying out airstrikes against the Syrian government in retaliation for the use of chemical weapons. An agreement was brokered with Russia that the Syrian government would hand over all stocks of chemical weapons (Houeix 2018). None the less, accusation of chemical weapons use continued. In April 2017, the new Trump administration bombed a Syrian air base in response to the alleged use of chemical weapons by the Syrian government (Houeix 2018). It was in response to the use of chemical weapons in April 2018 that Britain, France and America decided to launch air strikes (Houeix 2018).

The Syrian government had been besieging the area of Ghouta next to Damascus for several years. The area was held by Saudi sponsored Islamist militant group Jaish Al Islam (BBC 2018a). Jaish Al Islam had been launching attacks on Damascus from Ghouta for several years (Haaretz 2018). The Syrian government had begun an intense bombing campaign in early 2018 in order to retake Ghouta. For several weeks there had been negotiations between the Islamists and the Syrian and Russian governments with a deal being brokered whereby the Islamists would be allowed to leave Ghouta and travel to other Islamist held areas (Haaretz 2018). The evacuations of Islamist militants were already underway with only one or two groups refusing the deal. In the midst of this very intense situation, reports and footage emerged of children and adults being hosed down in a Ghouta hospital allegedly response to the use of chemicals, possibly chlorine (Shaheen 2018).

The alleged chemical attacks occurred on Saturday 7 April. There was immediate controversy with the Syrian government claiming that it had not used any chemical weapons (Shaheen 2018). The Russian government also claimed that no chemical weapons had been used and that there had been a staged event by Jaish Al Islam (BBC 2018b). Initial reports of the event were inconclusive. For example, the regularly cited Syrian Observatory for Human Rights was quoted stating that people had suffered from suffocation after conventional weaponry usage (Reuters 2018a). Two days after the attack the Syrian government and Russia asked the Organisation for the Prevention of Chemical Weapons (OPCW) to come into Ghouta to conduct tests (OPCW 2018).

France and Britain argued that there was no doubt that the Syrian government had used chemical weapons and that this act had to be punished. Both France and Britain said that they were ready to act (Chrisafis 2018; Veselinovic and Vonberg 2018). America also stated that were it to be established that the Syrian government had used chemical weapons America too would punish the Syrian government. The week following the alleged chemical weapons attack and the news was dominated by the chemical weapons attack and the threatened strikes from France, Britain and America.

Russia in response warned that if any Russian personnel were hurt or killed Russia would retaliate militarily (Embury-Dennis 2018). Whilst this drama was unfolding, polls taken of British public opinion showed that the majority of the British public did not support military action in Syria (YouGov 2018). Theresa May did not recall Parliament to authorise the airstrikes which were launched very early in the morning of 14 April, the night before the day on which the OPWC were due to arrive in Damascus.

The impact of the strikes on the Syrian government's chemical weapons capacities is uncertain. A building was hit as part of the strikes that had been verified by the OPWC as free from chemical weapons (for an overview see BBC 2018c). American statements after the strikes said that all chemical capacities had been destroyed (BBC 2018c). Shortly afterwards however the Pentagon then stated that perhaps not all of Syria's chemical weapons capacity had been wiped out (Burns 2018). Given that chlorine was claimed to have been used it would be unlikely that this standard domestic use and legal chemical would be eradicated.

The British Government's Justification for Not Consulting Parliament

Prime Minister Theresa May made a decision to launch the airstrikes without asking for Parliamentary authorisation prior to the military action. In the days running up to the strikes, Members of Parliament

(MPs) on both sides of the House argued that May needed to ask for Parliamentary authorisation for any military action (Walker 2018). The Prime Minister chaired an emergency Cabinet meeting on Thursday 12 April but did not call upon Parliament.

After the bombing, May initially set out her reasons for not recalling Parliament in the House of Commons on 16 April:

> ...why did we not recall Parliament? The speed with which we acted was essential in co-operating with our partners to alleviate further humanitarian suffering and to maintain the vital security of our operations. This was a limited, targeted strike on a legal basis that has been used before. And it was a decision that required the evaluation of intelligence and information, much of which was of a nature that could not be shared with Parliament. We have always been clear that the Government have the right to act quickly in the national interest. I am absolutely clear, Mr Speaker, that it is Parliament's responsibility to hold me to account for such decisions, and Parliament will do so. But it is my responsibility as Prime Minster to make these decisions—and I will make them. [Hon. Members: "Hear, hear!] (HC Deb, 16 April 2018, Col 43)
>
> Also,
>
> In observing the convention, we must ensure that the ability of our armed forces to act quickly and decisively, and to maintain the security of their operations, is not compromised. (HC Deb, 16 April 2018, Col 51)

A far more detailed rationale was given the following day in the Emergency Debate held on the 17 April 2018. The full debate is transcribed in HC Deb, 17 April 2018, column numbers will be given below from the debate. The leader of the Labour opposition, Jeremy Corbyn, tabled the Emergency Debate and argued that there should be a statutory basis for Parliament to authorise military action (Col 195).

May in turn recognised the Parliamentary convention but argued that the government had been right to not adhere to it for the April airstrikes. May cited the Cabinet Manuel of 2011 and Fallon's written answer of 2016 that in essence, the government reserved the right to not follow the convention when it would not be appropriate

> The exception to the convention is important to ensure that this and future Governments can use their judgment about how best to protect the security and interests of the UK. In observing the convention, we must ensure that the ability of our armed forces to act quickly and decisively,

> and to maintain the security of their operations, is not compromised...If we were to attempt to clarify more precisely circumstances in which we would consult Parliament before taking military action, we would constrain the operational flexibility of the armed forces and prejudice the capability, effectiveness or security of those forces. (Col 200)

May set out when she believed the convention was applicable, arguing that the convention was relevant for large scale offensive military operations:

> There are situations—not least major deployments like the Iraq war—when the scale of the military build-up requires the movement of military assets over weeks, and when it is absolutely right and appropriate for Parliament to debate military action in advance, but that does not mean that that is always appropriate. This therefore cannot and should not be codified into a parliamentary right to debate every possible overseas mission in advance. (Col 204)

May then set out four 'fundamental reasons' why the convention was not relevant for the action: effectiveness; protecting intelligence; the need to work closely with allies and to keep allied plans secret; that there was an existing legal basis for the intervention already, that of humanitarian emergency. May also argued that the military action the government had just taken demonstrated that putting the Convention on a statutory footing would stop Britain from being able to act flexibly (Col 205–208).

Effectiveness

The first 'fundamental reason' given by May was there was an overwhelming need for surprise, speed and uncertainty. May particularly stressed that a Parliamentary debate would have compromised the military operations, stating to Parliament that a debate would have necessitated revealing military targets in advance. May stressed the elements of surprise and uncertainty that were key to the operation in order for the military action to be effective and to ensure security of the military, but also so that the Syrian government could not take measures to mitigate against the strikes.

May also categorically told the House that the Syrian government was unaware of any military plans for the operation:

> In the case of our actions last weekend, the Syrian regime has one of the most sophisticated air defence systems in the world today. To counter such a system, it is vital to confuse the enemy as much as possible and to conceal the timing and targets of any planned attack. For example, if they had known even the category of target we had identified—in other words, our narrow focus on chemical weapons—that would have allowed them to concentrate rather than disperse their air defences. They could also have pre-empted our attack by dispersing their chemical weapons stocks, instead of leaving them at the target sites that we had identified.
>
> Our ability to exploit uncertainty was a critical part of the operation, and that uncertainty was also a critical part of its success. We know that the Syrian regime was not aware in advance of our detailed plans. If I had come here to the House to make the case for action in advance, I could not have concealed our plans and retained that uncertainty. I would quite understandably have faced questions about the legality of our action. The only way I could have reassured the House would have been to set out in advance—as I did yesterday after the event—the limited, targeted and proportionate nature of our proposed action. I would have faced questions about what aircraft and weapons we were planning to use, when the operation was going to take place, how long it was going to last and what we were going to do.
>
> All of that would have provided invaluable information that would have put our armed forces at greater risk and greatly increased the likelihood of the regime being able to shoot down our missiles and get their chemical weapons away from our targets. I was not prepared to compromise their safety and the efficacy of the mission. *[Interruption.]* To the shadow Foreign Secretary, who from a sedentary position is saying that it is nonsense to argue about the security of our armed forces, I say that that should be at the forefront of our thinking. (Col 205)

Protecting Intelligence

The second fundamental reason was that of protecting intelligence. May explained at length that a Parliamentary debate would have necessitated sharing intelligence-based information with Parliament. This reason is also related to the rational of 'effectiveness' and not revealing to the Syrian government where the military strikes would occur. This was mentioned in the debate on 16th April but explained at length on 17 April:

> It is not possible to bring all the intelligence through to this House; it is not possible to make all that intelligence public. Sometimes, actually, more information can be made available after the event than in advance of the event, because we do need to maintain the operational security of our armed forces. (HC Deb, 16 April 2018, Col 59)
>
> The second reason is the nature of the information that I see as Prime Minister, along with the National Security Council and the Cabinet. The Government make use of a wide range of sources of information, both those in the public domain and secret intelligence. In this case, drawing on the lessons of the past, we made a rigorous assessment of the available open-source material and intelligence about the Douma attack. Indeed, when my hon. Friend the Member for Gainsborough (Sir Edward Leigh) looked me in the eye and asked me to tell him that it was the Syrian regime that was responsible, I could do so in part because of the intelligence and assessment I had seen, and because I had discussed that intelligence and assessment with senior security and military officials, the National Security Council and Cabinet.
>
> In the post-Iraq era, it is natural for people to ask questions about the evidence base for our military actions, including when we cite intelligence. They want to see all the information themselves. But we have an obligation to protect the safety and security of our sources. We must maintain secrecy if our intelligence is to be effective now and in the future. We have obligations to our partners to protect the intelligence they share with us, just as they protect intelligence we share with them, and we have to be judicious even in explaining the types of intelligence we use in any given case, or risk giving our adversaries vital clues about where our information comes from. (HC Deb, 17 April 2018, Col 206)

The Need to Work Closely with Allies

The third 'fundamental reason' given by May was the need to work together with Britain's closest allies. This reason was rather briefly explained and is not necessarily separable from the first two:

> That was firmly in the British national interest. Working together with America and France, and doing so at pace, was fundamental to achieving that effect.

> If I had come to the House in advance of this operation to set out the totality of our effort, I would also have had to share with Parliament the breadth of our allies' plans, for this was a combined operation where the totality of our effort was key to delivering the effect. Not only would this have constrained their flexibility to act swiftly, but it would have fundamentally undermined the effectiveness of their action and endangered the security of our American and French allies. (Col 207/208)

Legality

The final fundamental reason given by May was that the action was an existing legal (international law) basis for the intervention already, that of humanitarian emergency. May situated the action in what she argued was a legal tradition beginning with the first Gulf War and the establishment of no-fly zones in Iraq, and included the intervention in Kosovo in 1999. The action, May argued was right and legal because it was necessary, proportionate and the last resort. These three criteria May argued meant that the action qualified under international law.

> The fourth reason is that the legal basis for UK action has previously been agreed by Parliament. As the hon. Member for Ilford South (Mike Gapes) said so movingly during the statement yesterday, there is a long tradition on both sides of this House that has considered that military action on an exceptional basis—where necessary and proportionate, and as a last resort—to avert an overwhelming humanitarian catastrophe is permissible under international law. The three criteria that I set out in my statement yesterday are the same three criteria used as the legal justification for the UK's role in the NATO intervention in Kosovo. As I also explained, our intervention in 1991 with the US and France and in 1992 with the US to create safe havens and enforce the no-fly zones in Iraq following the Gulf war were also justified on the basis of humanitarian intervention. (Col 208)

The government also published what it stated was the legal advice that it had been given about the strikes and international law:

> The UK is permitted under international law, on an exceptional basis, to take measures in order to alleviate overwhelming humanitarian suffering. The legal basis for the use of force is humanitarian intervention, which requires three conditions to be met:

> (i) There is convincing evidence, generally accepted by the international community as a whole, of extreme humanitarian distress on a large scale, requiring immediate and urgent relief;
> (ii) It must be objectively clear that there is no practicable alternative to the use of force if lives are to be saved; and
> (iii) The proposed use of force must be necessary and proportionate to the aim of relief of humanitarian suffering and must be strictly limited in time and in scope to this aim (i.e. the minimum necessary to achieve that end and for no other purpose). (BBC 2018d)

In answer to a written question from Lord Truscot, Lord Ahmad (the Foreign Office Minister of State for the Commonwealth and UN) also stressed that the strikes had been carried out as 'last resort' (HL Written Answers, 16 April 2018). Presumably, this is a reference to point ii of the legal advice published by the government. In answer to another written question, Lord Ahmad explained that the government's action had been permitted under international law (HL Written Answers, 17 April 2018).

In addition to the claims about the existing legal basis for the strikes, May also made another argument that waiting for a UN Security Council Resolution (an action that would confer international legality under the UN Charter) was no longer acceptable to Britain due the potential for a Russian veto:

> May warned: "The leader of the opposition has said that he can 'only countenance involvement in Syria if there is UN authority behind it'. The house should be clear that would mean a Russian veto on our foreign policy." (Crerar and Elgot 2018)

Evaluating the Government's Reasons for Not Asking Parliament for Authorisation

The British government did not ignore the Parliamentary convention as such. Rather, May made an argument based on four reasons as to why the Parliamentary convention did not apply in this particular case. The parameters of the Parliamentary convention, as explained by Fallon in 2016 and by May above, do allow for the government in essence to determine what is necessary for 'effectiveness' and security.

In terms of the claims that the action was justified under existing international law, this is irrelevant for the Parliamentary convention. The Parliamentary convention is about *domestic* authorisation of action.

Whilst international legality may well play an important, or even crucial part, in domestic political debate on a proposed action, it is not to be assumed that there is any automatic relationship between that and Parliamentary backing for military action. It is perfectly possible to envisage a proposed action that may be legal in international terms but not agreed to by Parliament. Indeed, this could be argued to be the case for Cameron's proposed military action against the Syrian government in 2013, given that the circumstances were exactly the same as they were in April 2018. However, despite this, Cameron still chose to go to Parliament to ask for authorisation. Below we consider May's arguments in their own terms.

Effectiveness and Protecting Intelligence

As explained above, the first 'fundamental reason' given by May for not asking Parliament to authorise the military action was there was an overwhelming need for surprise, speed and uncertainty. This was argued to be important both in terms of a swift reaction but also in terms of the security of the British operation and military personnel and also of not weakening the effectiveness of the operation. Time and publicity, in essence, May argued would be highly detrimental to the overall effectiveness of the air strikes. This argument is not supported however by the actions of Britain's partners.

Firstly, the question of the necessity for speed does not in itself rule out convening Parliament. In the run-up to the strikes there were calls for Parliament to be convened and to vote on the issue from Labour and Conservative MPs and also the Labour leader (Walker 2018). Thus Parliamentarians did not seem to think that short notice was a barrier. There does not seem to be any obvious reason why Parliament should not be reconvened however short the time scale.

Secondly, when considering the question of speed in relation to security and secrecy, it would be difficult to avoid the matter of Donald Trump the American president's tweets. Well known for his tweeting, the period between the alleged chemical attacks and the British, French and American air strikes was impressive even by Trump's normally high octane output. Initially, Trump did not tweet at all, reflecting a fairly low key reaction in the White House. After a couple of days however Trump began to tweet often, directly blaming Assad and calling him an 'animal' and also blaming Russian President Putin for the chemical attacks.

Trump caused international consternation with his tweets on the morning of 11 April, promising Russia that American missiles were on their way to Syria:

> Russia vows to shoot down any and all missiles fired at Syria. Get ready Russia, because they will be coming, nice and new and "smart!" You shouldn't be partners with a Gas Killing Animal who kills his people and enjoys it! (Vasquez and Hansler 2018)

However, on the same day General James Mattis the US Secretary of Defence claimed that the US was still assessing the intelligence as to the provenance of the chemical weapons (Vasquez and Hansler 2018). The following day President Trump tweeted:

> Never said when an attack on Syria would take place. Could be very soon or not so soon at all! In any event, the United States, under my Administration, has done a great job of ridding the region of ISIS. Where is our 'Thank you America?' (Walker 2018)

At the same time, American newspapers were reporting that there were intense disagreements between the White House and Pentagon in relationship to the scale and aim of the proposed strikes. It was reported in the run-up to the strikes (and after) that Secretary of Defence James Mattis had argued against White House desires for more extensive strikes against the Syrian air force (Cooper et al. 2018). In the week before the strikes, Russian newspapers were reporting that America would notify Russia of the location of strikes (Lockie 2018).

The Telegraph also reported that Russia and America were coordinating the planned airstrikes (Rayner et al. 2018). The day before the strikes The Telegraph reported that the American–Russian coordination was explained to the British Cabinet in order to assure them that any British military action would not spiral into a confrontation with Russia (Rayner et al. 2018). In the end the air strikes were limited. Mattis called the strikes 'show strikes' (Kheel 2018), that is strikes that 'sent a message' but that were limited in terms of damage done. What was notable was that there were no casualties resulting from the airstrikes, military or civilian, Syrian or Russian.

After the strikes, the White House denied there had been any cooperation with Russia over the strike (Jacobs 2018). However, the French

Defence Minister Florence Parly informed the French Parliament that Russia *had* been notified in advance of where the strikes would be (Al Jazeera 2018). Reuters reported a statement from an unnamed official that the strike targets had been evacuated well in advance of the strikes because of Russian notification (Reuters 2018b). Russian Foreign Minister Sergei Lavrov stated the following week that there had been discussions between Russian and American officials about the strikes and that Russia had told America of Russia's 'red lines' in terms of where not to strike (Sky 2018).

It is not possible to say with absolute certainty if Russia and America did negotiate the strikes in advance. Given the limited nature of the strikes, the lack of casualties and the French government's statement and media reports, it is a reasonable assumption that there was a significant amount of communication between Russia and America and France in the run-up to the strikes. By extension, the Syrian government would also have been informed. Such is the military relationship between Russia and Syria in Syria that Russian military advisors are embedded with most Syrian army units (TASS 2017). The advantage to world peace of the pre-strike notifications was that there was no clash between nuclear powers, for which we can all be grateful.

However, to return to the question of British Parliamentary authorisation of military action the point is that May argued for secrecy on the basis that the Syrian state could not know anything about the strikes. May *categorically* told Parliament that the Syrian government was unaware of any military plans for the operation. Yet we are left with the curious idea that the strikes could not be discussed with Parliament in order to maintain secrecy, but meanwhile the 'enemy', i.e. the Syrian state in this case, was most likely in possession of the information anyway. The concept of 'show strikes' and whether the UK should participate in such a thing would certainly be worth debating in Parliament.

Legality and Humanitarian Emergency

A key part of May's justification for not asking Parliament to authorise the military action was that it was legal under existing international humanitarian law and that this law had served as a basis for previous British military actions. As argued above, whether a military action is legal in terms of international law is as a matter of fact irrelevant for the Parliamentary convention. It may well be very important for garnering

Parliamentary support for a proposed action but that is an entirely different matter. The Parliamentary convention is about domestic authorisation not international. Thus there were concerns raised about the new Parliamentary Convention and the potential impact on Britain's international agreements, for example, what if Parliament voted against proposed military action that would be part of a NATO action or a UN Security mandated operation (see references in Chapter 2 from people worrying about Britain becoming irrelevant on the world stage, e.g. Gaskarth 2016).

However, it is worth considering this argument on its own terms. May argued that there was a tradition of humanitarian intervention based on international law. May cited the First Gulf War and the establishment of 'no-fly zones' in Iraq and also the Kosovo intervention in 1999 as precedents. However, the facts do not support May's arguments. The first Gulf War 'no-fly zone' in 1991 was in fact established by the UN Security Council under United Nations Security Council Resolution 688 (BBC 2002). It is the case that the justification *was* humanitarian but the action was authorised by the UN Security Council in the name of international peace and security (the UNSCR may be read here UN 1991).

This then is the legal basis for the Iraq 'no-fly zone'. The broader development of the doctrine of humanitarian intervention is complex and it is not the case that there is a recognised basis in international law for humanitarian intervention. During the 1990s there was much international argument about a 'developing norm' of humanitarian intervention. Critics worried about the potential for great power abuse if key UN Charter norms of non-intervention and sovereignty were jettisoned (for example Nambiar 1999) whilst supporters stressed that major human rights abuses that 'shocked the conscious of mankind' (Annan 1999) could simply not be allowed to keep occurring.

The 1999 Kosovo intervention conducted by NATO is widely held to be a successful humanitarian intervention, however, it is also illegal in terms of international law, i.e. it lacked UN Security Council authorisation. It was conducted by NATO because Russia had made it clear that it would not support military intervention and would use its UN Security Council veto. Thus the report of the Independent International Commission on Kosovo concludes that the intervention was illegal but legitimate (OUP 2000: p 4). The House of Commons also found that the intervention was illegal but moral (House of Commons 2000).

It was partly due to contestation about humanitarian intervention in Kosovo (OUP 2000: p 10) that the International Commission on Intervention and State Sovereignty was established and in 2001 published a very significant report entitled *The Responsibility to Protect* (ICISS 2001). *The Responsibility to Protect* (commonly shortened to the R2P) attempted to overcome the controversies generated by humanitarian intervention through establishing a number of necessary criteria for an intervention (ICISS 2001). The R2P also stressed that the concept of sovereignty need to be redefined in order to overcome the 'rights v sovereignty' impasse that had dominated the debate in the 1990s (ICISS 2001: paragraph 2.4).

The Libyan intervention in 2011 is argued to represent an example of the R2P in action, as the argument that the Libyan government was responsible for its people was cited in the UN Security Council resolution 1973. However, what is also of note is that this intervention was initially authorised by a UN Security Council resolution, 1973 (Hehir 2013). Russia and China abstained rather than vetoed, which meant in essence supporting the initial action. However, the transformation of the intervention into an operation to depose Gaddafi was controversial (Zenko 2016). The R2P has remained a contested concept as has humanitarian intervention more broadly. For an excellent overview of the various legal and political arguments on the topic, see Ware (2018). There is no clear legal or political consensus on the matter of humanitarian intervention (Ware 2018: 9). Thus the argument made by the government that there is an existing legal basis for humanitarian intervention does not hold.

The legal basis given by the British government also suggests that humanitarian intervention must be the 'last resort' (also stressed in the original R2P report). This is difficult to sustain given the events in the UN following the chemical attacks. The UN Security Council discussed two draft resolutions on the chemical attacks, one put forward by America and a counterproposal put forward by Russia (UN 2018). The American proposal would have established a mechanism whereby the UN could (following investigation) apportion responsibility for the attacks. The Russian proposal also sought to establish an investigatory mechanism but proposed that this could not apportion responsibility.

Sweden, a non-permanent member of the UN Security Council, stressed that the disagreement did not mean that the Council should give up and that as a first step the OPCW should be allowed to begin work

(UN 2018). The Swedish representative also stressed that the Security Council impasse did not mean that international law had failed but that more discussions were needed (AFP/The Local 2018). The Syrian representative also stated at the meeting that his government had officially invited the OPCW into begin work (UN 2018). The strikes came on the night before the day during which the OPCW was to arrive.

The British government furthermore, as discussed above, seemed to reject the idea of the UN Security Council veto in general. It is certainly true, as May argued, that accepting the validity of the UN Security Council veto does in principle mean that Russia (or indeed China or America or French) can veto British foreign policy. But so too does that veto allow Britain to veto Russian or Chinese or French foreign policy. This is not a new development but the premise of the UN Security Council which has underpinned the post-World War II international order.

Since 1945 and the establishment of the UN Charter, states have agreed that there are limits to what are legitimate foreign policy actions. Certain foreign policy actions are to be ruled out of the bounds of what is considered legitimate, particularly when it comes to the use of force against other states which is only considered to be legitimate in certain very limited circumstances. The very basis of the UN Charter is that of limiting interstate conflict. Thus, May is correct, agreeing to abide by the rules established the UN Charter *does* limit foreign policy in that states sign up and agree to refrain from certain types of behaviour in the international realm, in particular that relating to intervention. Indeed, this is precisely why the question of humanitarian intervention has remained problematic and controversial (see the R2P second volume; also see Ware 2018).

However, to argue that this is a problem and the British government should have a free hand as and where it wishes is a profound blow to any sense of the international rules-based order. International law, or the agreed framework within which states can act permissibly in terms of interstate behaviour, does not change depending upon who is doing the 'acting'. Or to put it another way, the rules apply to all equally or they cease to apply.

Another reason given for the speed of the strikes, and therefore the impossibility of recalling Parliament was the urgency of the situation in humanitarian terms. The idea of acting to avert a humanitarian crisis is cited by Cameron to be a part of the convention. This justification would makes sense in the context of this being the only reported chemical attack since 2013 when the Syrian government had allegedly destroyed all chemical weapons stocks. However, that is not the case. There was the infamous attack in April 2017 which also led to American strikes and other alleged uses of chemical weapons that were not reacted to. So in itself, this is an entirely selective reaction. There is also a legitimate question to be asked as to the extent of the humanitarian emergency created by these attacks. Whilst the Syrian conflict in itself has undoubtedly created a terrible humanitarian situation, with over half a million dead and millions displaced, there is no obvious rational for picking on another outrage in which 70 were killed as a trigger for intervention.

Moreover, after the 'show strikes' it was acknowledged that Syria still had the capacity to manufacture chemical weapons, with the Pentagon stating shortly after the strikes that the Syrian government still had the capacity to make chemical weapons (for example, Gibbons-Neff 2018). Indeed the Ghouta attack had been with chlorine, a common chemical used in manufacturing and domestic contexts. Thus it is highly unlikely that anything short of major countrywide bombardment could destroy all national stocks of chlorine.

Parliament's Response to the Air Strikes

As discussed above, the leader of the Labour opposition, Jeremy Corbyn, tabled the Emergency Debate on April 17 and argued for Parliament to have much stronger powers for authorising war. Corbyn also tabled a motion that would allow for a retrospective vote of disapproval on government action. In the convoluted way of Parliamentary business, the motion proposed by Corbyn was, 'That this House has considered Parliament's rights in relation to the approval of military action by British Forces overseas' (HC Deb, 17 April 2018, Col 192). With the intention that MPs who felt that Parliament had *not* had its rights respected could vote *against* the motion.

The motion however was passed by 317 votes to 256. To translate this from Parliamentary procedure into something understandable, this meant that 317 MPs voted in support of the motion. This said, in as many words, that those MPs felt that the government had done all that was needed in terms of respecting Parliamentary rights, i.e. those MPs did not feel that the government needed to have gone further and asked for authorisation before any military action.

Conclusion

Theresa May made a detailed argument about why the government did not need to ask Parliament in order to authorise the military action against Syria. Firstly May stressed that in general the Parliamentary convention applied to large scale military operations such as Iraq (HC Deb, 17 April 2018, Col 204, and also see Ziegler 2019: 7). The weight of the arguments made by May fell upon the need for effectiveness in particular with reference to secrecy for security and operational reasons.

The reality of the action however was one that had been publically discussed for a week and moreover, and more crucially, Russia was informed in advance in order to avoid a dangerous escalation. These were 'show strikes' that damaged a couple of evacuated facilities and left the Syrian government's capacities untouched. The legal basis was also not as the government portrayed it. At best, humanitarian intervention is a contested idea and it is simply not the fact that there is non-contested legal basis for humanitarian action. The action also did not meet the government's own criteria for humanitarian action, for example urgency and last resort.

The justifications for the Syria strikes do not stand up in their terms. Looking back at the sequence of events as documented in the media at the time, it would appear that France and Britain made a decision to launch airstrikes. America was unsure initially and France and Britain then waited until America had made a decision about participation and the level of strikes to be launched. Thus in principle, Britain could have, without Parliamentary authorisation, become involved in a much greater military operation potentially leading to conflict with Russia. As the events unfolded in practice, Britain engaged in what could reasonably be called 'virtue signaling' with bombs at a cost of several million pounds. Again, probably a hard sell to the House of Commons. All in all, the episode reflects very badly on the government and suggests some dishonesty in terms of May's arguments to Parliament on 17th April.

It is a serious matter that the government participated in military strikes that they could not justify even after the fact. It is in fact precisely in these kinds of circumstances that Parliamentary authorisation is required in order to domestically legitimate military action. It can be hypothesised that the government chose not to go to Parliament because it had decided to conduct these air strikes. Had the government gone to Parliament they would have been asked to discuss the risk of a greater conflagration with Russia. They then would have been forced to justify why this risk was worth it in the context of the broader catastrophe of the Syria war. Had they assured the House of Commons that there was no risk of escalation with Russia, they would have had to explain to the House of Commons that Britain had been asked to engage in a 'show strike'. A kind of posturing but with real bombs for various reasons but clearly none to do with actual military or strategic rationale or indeed, British interests.

Last but not least, it is also important to note that the intervention did not have the support of the majority of British people. Thus to compound the misinformation, this was military action taken against the wishes of the majority of the public. It would seem that this is exactly the kind of military adventurism that the new Parliamentary convention was designed to overcome. As mentioned above, Cameron went to Parliament to ask for authorisation of exactly the same kind of action, limited airstrikes, in which there was a far smaller risk of escalation as it was before Russian involvement.

In the week following the airstrikes, Parliament was given the opportunity to hold the government to account and assert itself. It did not do so however. Parliament could have retrospectively criticised the government and asserted its rights. However, for a number of no doubt local political reasons Parliament did not do this. Rather, Parliament chose to support the government in the government's avoidance of the Parliamentary convention.

This then suggests a failure of Parliament to hold the government to account and to assert its own rights. Parliament failed here to reflect public wishes to avoid military intervention. The problem then is raised not so much of an assertive executive but of a weak legislature that refuses to do what it should be doing and is entitled to do and furthermore ignores the wishes of the electorate.

References

AFP/The Local. (2018, April 12). What the Syrian People Want and Need Is Peace and Justice: Swedish Ambassador. *The Local Sweden*. Available from https://www.thelocal.se/20180412/what-the-syrian-people-want-and-need-is-peace-and-justice-sweden-security-council.

Al Jazeera. (2018, April 14). *Syria's War: France Rules Out Confrontation with Russia*. https://www.aljazeera.com/news/2018/04/syria-war-france-rules-confrontation-russia-180414063828974.html.

Annan, K. (1999, September 18–24). Two Concepts of Sovereignty. *The Economist*, pp. 81–82.
BBC. (2002, September 9). *UN Resolutions on Iraq*. Available from http://news.bbc.co.uk/1/hi/world/middle_east/2246037.stm.
BBC. (2018a). *House of Saud, Producer Michael Radford*. Available from https://www.bbc.co.uk/programmes/b09m53py.
BBC. (2018b, April 16). *Syria Air Strikes: Russia Denies Tampering with Suspected Chemical Attack Site*. Available from https://www.bbc.co.uk/news/world-middle-east-43783427.
BBC. (2018c, April 16). *US-Led Strikes on Syria: What Was Hit?* Available from https://www.bbc.co.uk/news/world-middle-east-43769332.
BBC. (2018d, April 14). *Syria Airstrikes the UK Government's Legal Position in Full*. Available from https://www.bbc.co.uk/news/uk-43768145.
Burns, R. (2018, April 15). Despite Strikes, Assad Retains Chemical Capability, Pentagon Admits. *The Times of Israel*. Available from https://www.timesofisrael.com/pentagon-despite-strikes-assad-still-has-chemical-weapons/.
Chrisafis, A. (2018, April 10). France Calls for Strong and United Response to Syria Chemical Attack. *The Guardian*. Available from https://www.theguardian.com/world/2018/apr/10/will-emmanuel-macron-enforce-red-line-syria-chemical-attack.
Cooper, H., Gibbons-Neff, T., & Baker, P. (2018, April 12). Mattis Tries to Put Brakes on Possible Syria Strike to 'Keep This From Escalating'. *The New York Times*. Available from https://www.nytimes.com/2018/04/12/us/politics/trump-syria-attack.html.
Crerar, P., & Elgot, J. (2018, April 16). Syria Strikes: May Tells MPs Britain Could Not Wait for UN Approval. *The Guardian*. Available from https://www.theguardian.com/politics/2018/apr/16/syria-strikes-may-tells-mps-uk-could-not-have-waited-for-un-approval.
Embury-Dennis, T. (2018, April 11). Russia Will Shoot Down Missiles Fired at Syria and Retaliate Against Launch Sites, Says Ambassador. *The Independent*. Available from https://www.independent.co.uk/news/world/middle-east/russia-us-missiles-syria-launch-sites-lebanon-zasypkin-putin-a8298941.html.
Gaskarth, J. (2016). The Fiasco of the 2013 Syria Votes: Decline and Denial in British Foreign Policy. *Journal of European Public Policy, 23*(5), 718–734.
Gibbons-Neff, T. (2018, April 19). Missile Strikes Are Unlikely to Stop Syria's Chemical Attacks, Pentagon Says. *The New York Times*.
Haaretz. (2018, March 28). Saudi Backed Syrian Rebels Face a Stark Choice: Surrender to Assad or Die. *Haaretz*. https://www.haaretz.com/middle-east-news/syria/syrian-army-of-islam-faces-a-stark-choice-surrender-to-assad-or-die-1.5957469.
HC Deb. (2018, April 16). Vol 639, Col 39–92. Available from https://hansard.parliament.uk/Commons/2018-04-16/debates/92610F86-2B91-4105-AE8B-78D018453D1B/Syria.

HC Deb. (2018, April 17). Vol 639, Col 192–246. Available from https://hansard.parliament.uk/commons/2018-04-17/debates/EF164C0A-E0F5-40B6-A718-DD8693A2490C/MilitaryActionOverseasParliamentaryApproval.

HC Written Statement. (2016, April 18). HCWS678. Available from https://www.parliament.uk/written-questions-answers-statements/written-statement/Commons/2016-04-18/HCWS678.

Hehir, A. (2013). The Permanence of Inconsistency: Libya, the Security Council, and the Responsibility to Protect. *International Security, 38*(1), 137–159.

HL Written Answers. (2018, April 16). HL6958. Available from https://www.parliament.uk/business/publications/written-questions-answers-statements/written-question/Lords/2018-04-16/HL6958/.

HL Written Answers. (2018, April 17). HL7011. Available from https://www.parliament.uk/business/publications/written-questions-answers-statements/written-question/Lords/2018-04-17/HL7011/.

Houeix, R. (2018, April 16). *A History of the Syria Chemical Weapons 'Red Line'*. France 24. Available from http://www.france24.com/en/20180414-syria-chemical-weapons-red-line-obama-macron-assad-russia-usa-france-idlib.

House of Commons. (2000). *Foreign Affairs Committee, Fourth Report, Kosovo.* Available fromhttps://publications.parliament.uk/pa/cm199900/cmselect/cmfaff/28/2802.htm.

House of Commons. (2018, April 16). *Syria Debate.* https://hansard.parliament.uk/Commons/2018-04-16/debates/92610F86-2B91-4105-AE8B-78D018453D1B/Syria.

ICISS. (2001). *The Responsibility to Protect—Report of the International Commission on Intervention and State Sovereignty.* Ottawa: International Development Research Centre.

Jacobs, P. (2018, April 14). The US Says It Didn't Give Russia Any Advance Warning About Targets Hit in Syria Strikes. *Business Insider UK.* http://uk.businessinsider.com/us-russia-syria-strike-targets-no-advance-warning-2018-4?r=US&IR=T.

Kheel, R. (2018, April 13). Mattis Resists Trump's Calls for Larger Syrian Strike: Report. *The Hill.* Available from http://thehill.com/policy/defense/383107-mattis-halted-two-opportunities-to-strike-syria-this-week-report.

Lockie, A. (2018, April 12). Trump Will Reportedly Warn Russia Where in Syria the US Will Strike. *Business Insider UK.* http://uk.businessinsider.com/trump-will-reportedly-warn-russia-where-us-will-strike-in-syria-2018-4?r=US&IR=T.

Nambiar, S. (1999). NATO Celebrates Its Fiftieth Anniversary by Destroying Yugoslavia. *Mediterranean Quarterly, 10*(3), 15–24.

OPCW. (2018, April 10). *OPCW Will Deploy Fact-Finding Mission to Douma, Syria.* Available from https://www.opcw.org/news/article/opcw-will-deploy-fact-finding-mission-to-douma-syria/.

OUP. (2000). *The Kosovo Report, The Independent International Commission on Kosovo*. Oxford.

Rayner, G., Riley-Smith, B., & Luhn, A. (2018, April 13). US-Russia 'Hotline' for Syrian Airstrikes Could Help Avoid Conflict Esclating. *The Telegraph*. https://www.telegraph.co.uk/news/2018/04/12/us-russia-hotline-syrian-air-strikes-could-help-avoid-conflict/.

Reuters. (2018a, April 8). *Syria Says Ready to Start Rebel Talks After Alleged Gas Attack*. Available from https://www.reuters.com/article/us-mideast-crisis-syria-ghouta/syria-says-ready-to-start-rebel-talks-after-alleged-gas-attack-idUSKBN1HF074.

Reuters. (2018b, April 14). *Pro-Assad Official Says Targeted Bases Were Evacuated on Russian Warning*. Available from https://www.reuters.com/article/us-mideast-crisis-syria-assessment/pro-assad-official-says-targeted-bases-were-evacuated-on-russian-warning-idUSKBN1HL07R.

Shaheen, K. (2018, April 8). *Dozens Killed in Suspected Chemical Attack on Syrian Rebel Enclave*. Available from https://www.theguardian.com/world/2018/apr/08/syrian-government-accused-of-chemical-attacks-on-civilians-in-eastern-ghouta.

Sky News. (2018, April 21). *Russia: We Told US Where in Syria They Could Not Bomb*. Available from https://news.sky.com/story/russia-we-told-us-where-in-syria-they-could-not-bomb-11338625.

TASS. (2017, December 27). *Russian Military Advisors Work with All Syrian Army Units—Russian General Staff*. Available from http://tass.com/world/983232.

UN. (1991, April 5). *UNSCR 688*. Available at http://unscr.com/en/resolutions/688.

UN. (2018, April 10). *Security Council 8228th Meeting, SC/13288*. Available from https://www.un.org/press/en/2018/sc13288.doc.htm.

Vasquez, M., & Hansler, J. (2018, April 12). *Trump Taunts Russia, Says US Military Response Coming in Syria*. CNN. Available from https://edition.cnn.com/2018/04/11/politics/trump-missiles-tweet/index.html.

Veselinovic, M., & Vonberg, J. (2018, April 13). *Syrian Regime 'Highly Likely' to Blame for Chemical Attack, UK Says*. CNN. Available from https://edition.cnn.com/2018/04/12/middleeast/uk-france-support-us-syria-airstrikes-intl/index.html.

Walker, J. (2018, April 12). Theresa May Told She Must Ask Parliament Before UK Joins Attack on Syria. *Chronical Live*. Available from https://www.chroniclelive.co.uk/news/north-east-news/theresa-told-must-ask-parliament-14524618.

Ware, R. (2018, April 16). *The Legal Basis for Air Strikes Against Syrian Government Targets* (House of Commons Library Briefing Paper No. 8287).

YouGov. (2018, April 12). *By Two to One, the Public Oppose Missile Strikes on Syria*. Available from https://yougov.co.uk/news/2018/04/12/two-one-public-oppose-missile-strikes-syria/.

Zenko, M. (2016). *The Big Lie About the Libyan War, Foreign Policy*. Available from http://foreignpolicy.com/2016/03/22/libya-and-the-myth-of-humanitarian-intervention/.

Ziegler, K. (2019). The Use of Military Force by the United Kingdom, the Evolution of Accountability. In *The Oxford Handbook of Comparative Foreign Relations Law*. Oxford: Oxford University Press.

CHAPTER 5

British War Powers in Context and Conclusion

Abstract This final chapter is in two parts. This chapter situates Britain's war powers in the context of the war powers of other European states, in particular Germany and France. The second and final part of the chapter concludes the work. The work will argue that the convention needs to be put on a far more formal basis, for example statutory. However, the failure to even retrospectively criticise the government's refusal to recall Parliament in April 2018 suggests a democratic deficit at the heart of the British polity. Legislative control is only as good as the political will of the legislature. The British Parliament has to make a decision to play its constitutional role as the sovereign power in the state, a sovereign power that represents and acts on behalf of the citizens of the state.

Keywords Royal prerogative · Parliamentary convention · Syria · Foreign policy · Security policy

Introduction

This final chapter is in two parts. This chapter situates Britain's war powers in the context of the war powers of other European states, in particular Germany and France. The second and final part of the chapter concludes the work, considering what the position is with the Parliamentary Convention on war and what is the way forward.

T. McCormack, *Britain's War Powers*,
https://doi.org/10.1007/978-3-030-13682-6_5

British War Powers in Context

Until the adoption of the War Powers Convention in 2011, Britain had one of the weakest systems of democratic control over war powers. As the previous chapter has shown, the development of the British War Powers convention is a very particular reaction to political shifts in Britain after the end of the Cold War. The scope of differing legislative authority and constitutional powers in relationship to authorising war reflects differing constitutional and historical settlements and also recent political events in each state. As Ziegler argues (2019), comparisons in this area are limited given the differences in history, and political systems even of states that are democratic, which can mean many different configurations within a system (for an overview see Dieterich et al. 2010). However, as Ziegler (2019) goes on to argue, there *is* a marked post-Cold War trend in that we do see that there have been similar reactions to major military campaigns such as Iraq, the move to wars of choice and also broader trends in contemporary Western democracies and the need for legitimacy.

The rise in interest of the relationship between the legislature and the executive, and ultimately the public, and foreign and security policy, in particular the authorisation of war, is a topic that has become an area of interest with the end of the Cold War and a number of changes in foreign and security policy. As Wagner et al. (2017) have pointed out, the shift away from existential wars defending territory to 'wars of choice' (2017: 20) presents governments and society with a different discussion. Certainly this suggests that some of the Cold War assumptions about foreign policy, for example that 'politics stops at the waters edge' and that foreign policy has a kind of national, non-political imperative to it (Raunio and Wagner 2017: 1–2), as indeed it would in the context of an imminent attack on territory, are no longer relevant in an era in which war is framed as moral choice for saving strangers (ICISS 2001).

In this context also, as has been previously discussed, declarations of war are very rare, in particular given the post-WWII UN Charter successful reframing of war as an act of aggression and the main problem for international peace and security. Thus most post-Cold War interventions have not been framed as war and accompanied by a declaration but as humanitarian emergency and or self-defence, or in very broad abstract principles as defending the rules-based international order.

Related to the transformation of the way in which war is framed is a post-Cold War discussion about the 'democratic peace' (Dieterich et al. 2010). As Dieterich et al. have pointed out, ideas around the democratic peace have tended to treat democracies as homogenous things. Yet a key part of the democratic peace thesis is the argument that democracies are more likely to be more peaceful because of a number of internal structural things, for example, institutions that transmit public preferences more easily. Yet, as Dieterich et al. point out, how does this tally with democratic states in which foreign policy is very much as executive privilege? A related issue is that Western publics are generally consistently anti-war yet executives tend to be far more enthusiastic about military intervention. Scholarship developing the democratic peace thesis ideas has looked at different ways in which Parliaments control (or do not control) foreign policy with preliminary findings that increased Parliamentary involvement decreases military intervention (Dieterich et al. 2010 for an overview).

A commonality within European states has been that the end of the Cold War has precipitated a number of constitutional debates and changes. Germany for example participated in military action for the first time since the end of WWII. The Kosovo intervention although widely seen as a successful intervention raised disquiet in some European states both for the use of NATO and the principle of wars for human rights. Thus the idea of the 'wars of choice' has been important for precipitating discussion (Wagner et al. 2017). The Iraq intervention also has been very significant for recalibrating war powers, even in states that explicitly refused to take part in the Iraq intervention, for example. France also has undergone some constitutional amendments in terms of authorising war in reaction to contemporary conflicts and a broader sense of increasing democratic oversight in a modern democracy, as will be discussed below. As Raunio and Wagner (2017) argued recently, 'The observed trend towards stronger oversight is – in line with our second hypothesis – to a large extent explained by lack of trust in the executive'.

War Powers Across Europe

The following overview draws upon a number of sources including Dieterich et al. (2010), Ziegler (2019), and Ostermann (2017). Most notable in terms of major European states, is Germany, with very strong war powers (Wagner 2017). Finland also has very strong democratic control over war powers. Any type of military deployment outside of the case of an imminent attack must be authorised by the Finnish Parliament. Denmark also has strong Parliamentary control over war powers (Dieterich et al. 2010; Democratic Audit UK 2013). France like Britain has historically very weak democratic control over war powers. The French President Emmanuel Macron exercised his constitutional powers when he authorised France's Syria strikes without asking for Parliamentary authorisation. None the less, the strikes were criticised in France for a number of reasons including lack of Parliamentary authorisation (Bock 2018).

The section focuses in particular on Germany and France below, as both of these states are major powers and comparable to Britain in this way. Germany is the leading European power. France of course is also a nuclear power and has a seat on the UN Security Council. France, as does Britain, also has an Imperial past and guards its 'great power' status jealously.

Germany

Germany did not participate in the April 2018 air strikes against Syria. Following the airstrikes however there were reports in Germany that the German Defence Ministry was in discussion with American counterparts about joining future airstrikes if more chemical weapon attacks were to occur (Deutsche Welle 2017). Any potential action would have to be authorised by Parliament.

Germany has developed a set of Parliamentary war powers that are very comprehensive and cover virtually all possibilities. The specific context for this development in Germany has been the opposite to that in Britain, France and other states. Whereas in these states, war powers have been developed in order to constrain executive power, in Germany the dynamic has been a change in war powers in order to permit German military forces to engage in action outside of German. This has to be understood in the particular historical context for Germany.

The post-WWII German military was constitutionally prohibited from acting other than in defence of German territory (until 1990 West Germany). This is found in Article 87a of the Basic Law. The Basic Law, adopted and confirmed as the German Constitution in 1949 of the Federal Republic of Germany (then consisting of West Germany). However, Article 24 also allows for Germany to participate in collective security organisations. Although quite what this might be constitutionally permitted to entail and the question of what defence might mean was a matter of debate (Ziegler 2017). In was the political context of the post-War Germany that meant that the German army was assumed to be entirely defensive and participation in conflicts abroad almost inconceivable.

With the end of the Cold War came German reunification and the possibility of a very different kind of Germany in the near future. In the early 1990s Germany for the first time deployed armed forces outside of the UN (Ziegler 2019: 785).

> The first such mission concerned a maritime operation of NATO/WEU in 1992 to implement the embargo against the (then) Federal Republic of Yugoslavia imposed by UNSC Res 713 (1991) 'Socialist Federal Republic of Yugoslavia' (25 September 1991). The second deployment occurred in 1993 as part of integrated NATO-AWACS units (Airborne Warning and Control System) enforcing the no-fly zone imposed by UNSC Res 781 (1992) 'Bosnia and Herzegovina' (9 October 1992) and UNSC Res 816 (1993) 'Bosnia and Herzegovina' (31 March 1993) in the airspace over Bosnia-Herzegovina. The third deployment was to Somalia in 1993 as part of the UNOSOM II mission to provide military security for humanitarian assistance. (Ziegler 2017)

It was in response to these missions that Parliament itself challenged the Government and brought a case to the Constitutional Court: The Court's judgment was as follows:

a. First, it established that the German Constitution allowed for the deployment of Germany's armed forces abroad beyond the immediate defence of its territory, at least where such deployment occurred within a collective security system.
b. Second, the judgment established that the *Bundestag* (German Parliament) must consent to military deployments.
c. Third, the judgment contributed to the interpretation of the constitutional scope and limits of a transfer of sovereign powers in the context of international integration processes.
d. Fourth, the judgment is significant more generally for the relationship between the executive and parliament in the context of foreign affairs. (Ziegler 2017)

The 1994 court ruling stated that the German army was a Parliamentary Army (Wagner 2017). The German Parliament authorises *any* military action, whether that is something as a part of an international organisation such as NATO or not (Wagner 2017). This is a matter of dispute in British discussions, in particular the difficulties of having a statutory requirement in the event of participating in multilateral actions. In essence, Parliament must approve virtually all military deployments including small and low-risk ones, any change in mandate or continuation of mission. Exemptions are operations with special forces that require secrecy and participation in permanent multinational headquarters, notably however outside of a combat zone (Wagner 2017).

For Germany this Constitutional change (or perhaps clarification) can be understood in the context of a post-reunification discussion of becoming a 'normal' country. In particular participation in humanitarian interventions which were to some extent presented as an act of historical atonement for Germany (Borger 2012). Of note, that unlike what has occurred in Britain, this 1994 court decision was actually in order to *allow* Germany to participate in a legitimate (i.e. authorised) way in a military field which was still seen as very problematic in the context of German past (and particularly so in relationship to Yugoslavia much of which had been occupied by Nazi forces). By 1999 German planes were bombing Belgrade for the second time in half a century as part of the NATO coalition. As has been discussed in a previous chapter the NATO military intervention was without a UN Security Council Mandate and thus illegal in terms of international law (Deutsche Welle 2010). The German Parliamentary Participation Act of 2005 codified the constitutional rules on military action 'The consent requirement is triggered under the terms of the Act by the 'deployment of armed forces', which is further defined as 'involvement or anticipated involvement … in armed operations'. The risk of armed engagement is an indicator for when involvement may be anticipated'. (Ziegler 2019: 786). There is an exemption for emergency, the act requires an 'imminent danger, which allows no scope for delay' or 'operations whose purpose is to rescue persons from particularly dangerous situations, provided that the holding of a public debate in the Bundestag would endanger the lives of the persons in need of rescue' (Ziegler 2019: 787). With reference to the April air strikes and any further potential strikes, government spokesperson Steffen Seibert said that Parliament would vote on any operations, but that Parliament would be notified after the act if speedy action were required (Reuters 2018).

France

For France the discussion about war powers can also be located in the post-Cold War era. France, unlike Britain, did not participate in the Iraq War. A decision that at the time lead to much abuse being heaped upon France (Younge and Henley 2003). Traditionally France has had very weak democratic war powers. The decision to go to war has historically been seen as an entirely executive one. The French political system overall, specifically that of the Fifth Republic, established by De Gualle in 1985, is one in which the executive dominates.

> The constitution invokes the president as the guarantor of territorial integrity and treaties (art. 5) and as commander in chief (art. 15), whereas the government is responsible for the *organisation* of the armed forces (art. 34). e eminent personality of de Gaulle and his long-serving successors combined with these institutional and ideational dispositions to establish a practice of accepted presidential leadership. is forged a rather broad consensus on defence issues with little politicisation (Irondelle 2009: 118.; Rozenberg et al. 2011: 241). Hence, Vaïsse (2009: 16, 77) argues that foreign policy is the 'domaine régalien par excellence' of the president (cf. also Irondelle and Schmitt 2013: 128f.). Irondelle (2009: 129) characterises the French parliament as 'one of the most impotent parliaments in foreign and defense policies'. Born and Hänggi (2005) demonstrate that the French parliament lacks the powers of prior approval of missions and mandates. It also lacks the ability to influence a mission's duration. (Ostermann 2017: 102)

Whilst France did not suffer from the Iraq effect, there none the less was a discussion about constitutional powers that focused on reform and modernisation beginning with the Lamy Report. In 2008 however as a consequence of a reform commission set up by President Sarkozy and lead by former Prime Minister Edouard Balladur a new clause was introduced into Article 35 of the Constitution (Ostermann 2017: 102). Article 35 pertains to declarations of war, which as discussed previously are rare. The new clause stipulated that the Government would need to go to Parliament once it had decided to send armed forces abroad, at the latest three days following on from the start of the intervention.

However, whilst the new paragraph suggested a debate could be held, it also stipulated that there should not be a vote.

> ARTICLE 35.
> A declaration of war shall be authorized by Parliament.
> The Government shall inform Parliament of its decision to have the armed forces intervene abroad, at the latest three days after the beginning of said intervention. It shall detail the objectives of the said intervention. This information may give rise to a debate, which shall not be followed by a vote.
> Where the said intervention shall exceed four months, the Government shall submit the extension to Parliament for authorization. It may ask the National Assembly to make the final decision.
> If Parliament is not sitting at the end of the four-month period, it shall express its decision at the opening of the following session.

An English version of the French Constitution is available from *Conseil Constitutionnel France* website.

When France participated in the April 2018 airstrikes the French Parliament was not consulted beforehand, as is constitutionally right. There was no declaration of war in this case. Macron however was criticised for the action by both left and right politicians (Bock 2018). Betrand Badie for example argued in Le Monde that the bombing represented a 'logique dépassée' an anachronistic logic (Bock 2018). However, whilst the action was criticised there does not seem to be a discussion about removing war powers from the executive.

Conclusion

Who Governs?

This work has considered the development in Britain of a new Parliamentary convention on authorising war. There are two strands of conclusions discussed below. Firstly, this latest episode of the two decades-long wrangle over British war powers supports broader analysis from the literature on the problems of conventions and also work that has been done on the specific context for legislative power over the executive. Secondly, with reference to this specific case study, not only did the government argue that the convention was not applicable based on justifications that do not hold up to scrutiny but more importantly, there seemed to be little political will to hold the government to account. MPs did not punish the government for failing to consult Parliament in advance of military action that could have started a serious conflict in the region and globally, which was poorly justified and moreover that was not supported by the majority of the British public.

What Happened?

This convention seemed to be established firmly in 2013, and then 2015, when David Cameron went to Parliament to ask for authorisation for British airstrikes in Syria. In 2013, Parliament voted not to authorise airstrikes against the Syrian government in response to the use of chemical weapons. In 2015, Parliament voted to authorise British participation in coalition airstrikes against ISIS in Syria. Yet in April 2018, when faced with exactly the same circumstances as Cameron in 2013 and proposing exactly the same action, May chose not to ask Parliament for authorisation. Rather, May argued that the military action did not meet the criteria for the Parliamentary convention.

The reasons given by May, some of which have been understood to be exclusions from the convention, for example the necessity for secrecy, do not stand up to scrutiny given what is known about the matter. May categorically claimed after the strikes that the Syrian government did not have any information in the run-up to the military action. However, from media reports, the French statement and the total absence of casualties, it is very likely that Russia and France (with American backing) negotiated the strikes in advance so as to avoid military clashes. Syria would also then have been informed by Russia. Thus it seems very likely that the 'target' knew of the strikes but May claimed that Parliament could not know of any information.

Furthermore, if Cameron felt that the launching limited airstrikes with France and America in response to chemical weapons use needed Parliamentary authorisation, why is it that May did not? One main difference may well be that Cameron certainly expected to win the vote, he was very surprised that Parliament did not choose to authorise the airstrikes in 2013. May, coming after Cameron's venture, may well have worried that she would not win any vote given the similar circumstances and moreover that proposing to spend hundreds of thousands of pounds on 'show strikes' that also risked turning into a clash with Russia may well have been a hard sell.

That two different Prime Ministers from the same political party in the space of four years when confronted with the same situation acted in opposite ways suggests that the convention is at the very least, weak. Or rather, there is so much ambiguity in the convention as to render it more or less ineffective. As Mello and Strong argued in 2017, that the scope and range of the convention remain unspecified. Indeed as May argued in Parliament in April 2018, the government had pledged to adhere to the convention apart from when the government thought they should not.

The differences in the behaviour of the two Prime Ministers from the same party when faced with same situation, supports analysis more broadly on the role of the legislature in foreign policy. It is highly contextual and dependent on a number of factors. As Mello and Peters (2018: 3, 8) have argued;

> Case studies, however, suggest that the significance of parliaments in concrete cases often hinges not only on the extent of their formal authority but also on how the interaction with the executive plays out within this setting. Moreover, situational factors and how legislative–executive relations are man- aged often appear to be of high significance, but they have rarely been studied in detail…Born and Hänggi (2004, 2005) argue that opportunities for parliament to affect security policy result not only from its formal legal rights (authority). Rather, parliament's capability to become involved effectively ('ability', as in parliamentary resources like budget, staff, and infrastructure) and willingness of Members of Parliament (MPs) to conduct effective oversight (attitude) are important conditions as well.

The personality of the Prime Minister is also an important contextual facto, as Kaarbo has argued, This analysis is also illustrated by this specific case study. It is of note that Cameron not only went to Parliament to ask for authorisation for airstrikes twice but also committed the country to a referendum Scottish Independence, carried out in 2014, in which Scotland voted to remain part of the United Kingdom. Cameron also committed the country to a vote on whether to stay in the EU. A vote that Cameron also lost again much to his surprise. See also Strong on this subject of personality (2014).

To return to the discussion on conventions in chapter one, conventions are fundamentally political things that exist to the extent that they are adhered too. Strong (2018: 21) argues a powerful government could simply ignore the convention. However, the rise and fall of the Parliamentary convention suggests that it is not just about powerful governments, equally weak governments who might feel that they cannot make a case for proposed military action will chose to avoid asking Parliament for authorisation. Not only was May's government a minority one, but in this case May seems to have learnt the lesson from Cameron that when you ask for democratic authorisation for a political policy the answer may not be the one that you want.

Where then are we in terms of the British Parliamentary convention? As the current government has defined it, a convention that will be upheld when the government sees fit cannot really be said to exist, even allowing for the elastic nature of constitutional conventions (Fikfak and Hooper 2018). It would seem that thirteen years after the *Not in My Name* report and numerous Parliamentary and Lord's reports and academic analysis, we are still in a situation in which Parliamentary control over military action amounts to little more than heckling.

Yet beyond the confirmation of analysis of the specific context for effective legislative authority when it comes to foreign and security policy and also the inherent problems of constitutional conventions, another strand of analysis is confirmed by this episode. That is, as Jenkins (2007) argued in response to the 2006 report of the House of Lords Select Committee on the Constitution entitled *Waging War: Parliament's Role and Responsibility*, ultimately the question is one of political will. Constitutional and legislative constraints on executive behaviour are only as good as the political will to uphold them.

Despite the numerous Committees and discussions over the post-Iraq period, the British government has not felt under sufficient pressure to for example formalise the convention further (including in terms of clarifying the scope and range). Moreover, when given the chance to hold the government to account after the event by voting against the motion tabled by Jeremy Corbyn on Tuesday 17 April, MPs by a majority supported the government's policy of not recalling Parliament. Corbyn's motion, 'That this House has considered Parliament's rights in relation to the approval of military action by British Forces overseas. (HC Deb, 17 April 2018, Col 192)' was passed by 317 votes to 256 (as discussed in the previous chapter).

Meaning that the majority of MPs in the House of Commons believed that the government had done all that it needed to do in terms of 'respecting Parliamentary rights' and that the government did not need to ask for authorisation before such a military action. This then is the heart of the matter. Of course, MPs were voting after the event and war had (thankfully) not broken out between Russia and France, America and Britain. The strikes were lauded as a 'success' by Britain and America with claims that Syria's chemical weapons capacities had been destroyed and with no casualties. These claims were rapidly deflated within days and it should be remembered as discussed previously, the chemicals used were alleged to be chlorine, a common domestic and industrial chemical and thus stocks of which would remain under all but an attack entailing the carpet bombing of Syria.

As has been a point for discussion of the Parliamentary convention, timing of votes is important. The Iraq vote occurred as military action had more or less begun. A very different scenario to the 2013 Syria vote in which Cameron had allowed for a full and frank debate and in-depth consideration of consequences before any military action had begun. That MPs voted in support of government action after the event and when the action was seen to be successful does not support arguments made following the defeat of Corbyn's motion that it was clear that had the government asked Parliament for authorisation *before* the action, Parliament would have supported it.

The Parliamentary response then to the government's actions was weak. Despite the flimsiness of May's justifications, and indeed despite the fact that one of the most important arguments made by May in justification did not stand up to the known facts of the matter, MPs chose to support the government. MPs failed to understand or to take seriously, that there is a fundamental political question of legitimacy at stake. The MPs response demonstrates a kind of short-sighted pursuit of party political goals rather than thinking properly about Parliament's role in society. This also supports earlier points made about the day to day political limitations on MPs to really hold the government to account.

To return to Brazier's comment from the start of this work,

> How odd – perhaps bizarre – it is that the approval of both Houses of Parliament is required for pieces of technical, and often trivial, subordinate legislation, whereas it is not needed at all before men and women can be committed to the possibility of disfigurement or death. (Brazier 1999: 123)

Brazier's comment however does not cover the full potential of war. It is not just British armed forces that will be sent to their possible death but that military action is not a neat scientific experiment that can be finished when required. A country may become embroiled in a far greater conflict than envisaged, 'We must understand from previous conflicts that war is not some sort of hokey-cokey concept; once you're in, you're in', as Jim Sheridan memorably stated. Yet since the end of the Cold War, this is precisely how many powerful Western states have thought about war.

Since the end of the Cold War British, and Western government in general, have become used to the idea of 'wars of choice', wars waged against comparatively poor and weak states ostensibly in the name of human rights. Powerful states, whether in coalitions or international military alliances such as NATO, have intervened militarily and then withdrawn leaving the country to its fate. Libya for example is now home to a thriving ISIS community and slave markets following the Libyan intervention. Intriguingly contemporary articles that detail Libyan slave markets tend to leave out the role of the NATO intervention in destroying the state and creating a power vacuum (the slave markets became widely discussed late in 2017, see for example CNN 2017).

For much of the post-Cold War era powerful Western states played at war in a way that is reminiscent of Marie Antoinette playing at being a milkmaid in the purpose-built dairy and farm behind the walls of Versailles. But the era of 'wars of choice' in which powerful Western states got to play at resolving complex political problems and conflicts and then go home when they had had enough is ending. Russia agreed with the Syrian government to intervene militarily on behalf of the Syrian government against militant Jihadi groups, many of which had been externally sponsored and supported by America, Turkey and other states. Part of Russia's justification was that of a national interest to prevent Syria from becoming another Iraq or Libya and thereby opening a 'super-highway' as Aaron Stein has put it, to Jihadists to Turkey and the Caucasus (Stein 2018). Russia had initially supported the Libyan intervention (Russia abstained in the UN Security Council meeting rather than vetoed it) but turned against the intervention as the intervention itself spread into another regime change operation.

With the Syrian intervention Russia announced its return to the geopolitical arena. Ukraine is another case in point, where Russian annexation of Crimea and formenting of conflict in Donbass was a step to stop Crimea from drawing closer to the European Union and NATO.

Regardless of what one thinks about Russian actions (or indeed Western actions), the point is Western states will have less and less of a free hand to intervene where they will without potential clash with Russia, something that somewhat raises the stakes of an intervention. This is a reality that not all British politicians have grasped.

Moreover, it is not just Russia. It is a standard discussion now that there is a significant shift in geopolitics occurring with a relative decline in American power (not least of all amongst Western allies) and a more multipolar world order (or perhaps disorder) emerging. From France calling for a European army to defend against America to the Iran, Turkey, Russia Astana forum that has taken charge of the Syria war, it is a rapidly changing world. None of which is to say that the world order will be unrecognisable in the next ten years but simply that some central assumptions that guided foreign policy in the post-Cold War period need to be rethought.

In addition to the changing geopolitical order there is another related factor to consider in this context. As has been mentioned in several Parliamentary reports, declarations of war are very rare post-WWII. In her justification for not asking Parliament to authorise the April airstrikes against Syria, May argued that the Parliamentary convention was relevant for large scale pre-planned military operations such as Iraq (see previous chapter for references). This is untenable however. Firstly, Iraq style operations are less frequent with a noted shift post-Iraq to what Rogers' has termed 'remote control' war that avoid 'boots on the ground', for example airstrikes, drones, special forces and other forms of smaller scale military intervention (Rogers 2013). The assumption rests upon the notion that airstrikes or similar kinds of military intervention do not have the potential to spread or spill over into broader conflict and that therefore there is nothing existential at stake. As Jim Stewart and others have pointed out, military intervention is not like that. It is not a neat controllable thing with foreseeable outcomes.

Moreover, it rests on a strange assumption that how we define our intervention is how those on the receiving end will define it. A simple thought experiment suffices to demonstrate the limitations of this. If another government launched airstrikes on our military or chemical facilities we would absolutely treat it as an act of war, or if another government sent special forces into Britain or drone strikes or funnelled millions of pounds into anti-government militias, we would treat it as an act of war and retaliate. Western governments engaging in post-Cold War military interventions have lived in a strange alternate moral universe in which our military actions are always moral and justified and controllable, as if there was no existing state on the receiving end. States are increasingly favouring methods of intervention described by Rogers as 'remote control', eschewing large scale military operations and 'boots on the ground' in favour less visible means of intervention, special forces, funding proxies. The idea that the CIA's Operation Timbre Sycamore, that funnelled billions of dollars into anti-government militias in Syria, for example, should not be understood as an aggressive act akin to an act of war does not stand up to a minutes scrutiny. The point here is not to make the case about whether this was a good or bad strategy, but to make clear that limiting any convention or future statute to large scale military operations planned in advance means that most methods of contemporary warfare are simply excluded.

Moreover, and this is a fundamental point, British MPs knew that the majority of the British people *did not* support the military action whatever had happened in Syria with chemical weapons. This raises immediate questions about the relationship between MPs and the electorate but also further research questions for work on the relationship between democratic states and peaceful foreign policy. If the legislature and the executive simply ignore political preferences when it comes to foreign policy then the problem is elsewhere.

In summary, Britain seems to be in possession of a Parliamentary convention that means only what the government of the day says it means. Theresa May refused to ask Parliament to authorise military action of exactly the same sort and in response to the same things as Cameron's. May's justification did not stand up to serious scrutiny. MPs did not punish the government for failing to consult Parliament in advance of military action that could have started a serious conflict in the region and globally. Last but not least, the majority of British people were against the action.

Conventions are elastic and political things. Yet even by these problematic standards, it would be reasonable to argue that the Parliamentary Convention is so weak as to be almost irrelevant. A convention that relies entirely on whether the government sees fit to implement it can hardly be said to exist. Moreover, the Convention that the government acknowledges is one that applies to a very narrow type of military action, one that is decreasingly in evidence. The most important conclusion from the latest episode in April is that Parliament does not seem willing to hold the government to account about this.

Where to Next?

At the time of writing the Public Administration and Constitutional Affairs Committee are holding an inquiry into the role of Parliament in the UK Constitution. One of the issues to be considered is what role Parliament should play in authorising the deployment of military force. The inquiry has not been published as yet. Fifteen years after the Iraq war and numerous Parliamentary reports and inquiries, debates, scholarly analysis and three (Iraq and Syria) actual votes on military action, the question still stands. What role should Parliament play in authorising the deployment of military force?

At the heart of this question there is a fundamental question of legitimate authority in Britain. In Britain, the source of legitimate authority is the demos, the citizens of the country. Yet in this matter of potentially existential policy, the power remains in the hands of the executive. But democratic authority is not just exercised through rules and regulations whether constitutional or statutory, but also through Parliament holding the government to account by exercising it's authority over the executive. But democratic authority is not just exercised through rules and regulations whether constitutional or statutory, but also through Parliament holding the government to account by making sure the Government fulfils its democratic mandate. The latest episode in the rise and fall of the Parliamentary Convention reveals a democratic deficit at the centre of the most important policy realm of any state. Not only a formal democratic deficit, in that the convention can be ignored at will, but a more profound democratic deficit in that Parliament allowed it to happen and did not exercise even retrospective disapproval.

The executive has ignored public opinion and also, as illustrated by the April air strikes, engaged in potentially very risky military action on the basis of justifications that do not stand up to scrutiny. Unfortunately, in Britain previous governments have 'form' when it comes to misleading the public in foreign policy matters. The Chilcot Report and material released as part of the inquiry revealed quite an extraordinary level of manipulation and 'spin' and deliberate misleading in order to garner support for a military intervention.

In 2005, Jack Straw then Foreign Secretary made the following statement to the House of Commons Select Committee on Foreign Affairs:

> Unless we all start to believe in conspiracy theories and that the officials are lying, that I am lying, that behind this there is some kind of secret state

which is in league with some dark forces in the United States, and also let me say, we believe that Secretary Rice is lying, there simply is no truth in the claims that the United Kingdom has been involved in rendition full stop, because we have not been, and so what on earth a judicial inquiry would start to do I have no idea. (House of Commons 2006: Examination of Witnesses, Question 23)

In June 2018, the Intelligence and Security Committee published a report on role of British intelligence and security agencies in the American led system of extraordinary rendition. Extraordinary rendition is the system of illegal abduction, detention and transference of detainees to other countries for the purposes of interrogation and torture begun as part of the 'War on Terror' by the CIA and supported by other secret services and intelligence agencies including British. The report, which had been several years in the making, demonstrated that Jack Straw had most probably lied to Parliament and that British intelligence and security agencies had participated in extraordinary rendition with government knowledge (Intelligence and Security Committee 2018).

The point of these two examples is not to simply go over the foreign policy misdeeds of British governments but to make the point that it is a matter of historical and factual record that the British government has habitually mislead (to put it charitably) the public and Parliament when it comes to foreign policy. It is clear from the two reports mentioned above that Parliament, and other independent investigative bodies, e.g. the Iraq Inquiry commonly known by the name of the Chair, John Chilcot, do excellent work on scrutinising the government. Both of the reports mentioned above have reached extremely critical and damning conclusions about government behaviour and policies.

The problem is however that these are retrospective, seriously so, the damage is already done and ongoing. The Chilcot Report is to be lauded but it was published in 2016 and the Iraq War began in March 2003. Fourteen years after Jack Straw was a witness to the House of Commons Select Committee on Foreign Affairs we know that he probably lied to Parliament. Not only is the time lapse important but there are few if any consequences. Jack Straw for example did not even have to (or could not be compelled) give evidence to the Intelligence and Security Committee.

Thus as well as the fundamental question of legitimate authority over existential decisions, it is unfortunately the case that British governments have shown themselves to be untrustworthy on some very important foreign policy matters. Perhaps if we knew that our government would forever be run by saints from now on it would not matter. As this is unlikely to be the case however, we need a plan B.

Based upon the recent events in April the convention needs to be put upon a much firmer footing, ideally a statutory basis. One of the main arguments against a statute is that there is the possibility of the courts becoming involved on questions of the legality of a conflict (for example in terms of international law) or of the legality of conduct within the conflict. However, there is no rationale for thinking that this would be the case. Both of these questions are entirely separate to that of domestic authorisation of war (Mills 2018: 58). It may be the case that there is a greater willingness of courts to go to become involved in battlefield decisions as discussed by the Lords Constitutional Committee but this is a separate development. A statue would be relevant for the question of domestic authorisation military action.

An important matter that is clear from consideration of the events of April 2018 is that the scope of the convention needs to be much broader. The current government wishes to argue that the convention only applies in very limited circumstances, whereas the far more common ways in which successive governments have intervened militarily are excluded. This simply contradicts the raison d'etre of the convention in the first place. The convention is not a 'tick box' exercise but addresses a fundamental question of democracy.

Who in a democratic society should authorise war? The idea that launching airstrikes against another state (or sending drones or special forces or funding opposition militias for that matter) should be excluded from such authorisation because engaging in airstrikes is not an act of war is not tenable. Bombing another country is an act of military aggression, this is regardless of whether one thinks it is the morally right thing to do. So too are drone strikes or sending in special forces. If this were done to us, we would consider it an act of war. To deny this, is the excuse of a primary school child who seeks to wiggle out of blame by pointing out that they did not do exactly what they had been warned against doing, only something approximating it. Parliament certainly should be authorising such actions as sending special forces, regardless of the invitation, and the executive forced to explain its rational and strategy and final goals.

The convention needs to be established on a much firmer footing, preferably statutory and with a far wider scope specified than the current vague convention that essentially leaves it entirely to the discretion of the government to decide if and when the convention applies. Britain should follow the German model and establish Parliamentary authority over military deployments, whether unilateral or as part of a coalition, and included in this should be the use of drones, special forces and funding militaries. The point of consideration should not be the action itself, but the intent and the potential for escalation. If the intent is to intervene in a conflict (whether national or international) and alter the balance of forces therein, then Parliament should be asked to authorise it. Britain should follow the German Parliamentary Participation Act of 2005 'The consent requirement is triggered under the terms of the Act by the 'deployment of armed forces', which is further defined as 'involvement or anticipated involvement … in armed operations'. The risk of armed engagement is an indicator for when involvement may be anticipated'. (Ziegler 2019: 786).

There are no reasons, other than a lack of political will, that we cannot follow this comprehensive model. It is the case that as was bemoaned by many political figures in 2013 that it might mean that Britain cannot play the military role the government wishes to play. It is the case that it might meant that actions the government might think are morally right will not be authorised. It does not matter how bitterly the late Paddy Ashdown bemoans Britain's lost military influence in the world. It is not for the government to make these decisions.

However, ultimately this is something that rests with Parliament to push through. The failure to even retrospectively criticise the government's refusal to recall Parliament in April 2018 suggests a democratic deficit at the heart of the British polity. The general public did not support the military strikes. Yet MPs, who represent the demos, refused ultimately to assert their authority over the executive. Thus we arrive at the heart of the matter. Conventions, legislation and other forms of legislative control are only as good as the political will of the legislature. A hope for establishing the convention on a statutory footing would be that MPs would at least be forced to consider any military action in depth before the event. The government would be forced to justify itself. In order for any of it to happen however the British Parliament has to make a decision to play its constitutional role as the sovereign power in the state, a sovereign power that represents and acts on behalf of the citizens of the state.

References

Bock, P. (2018, April 17). Macron's Bid to Look Strong on Syria Could Weaken Him in France. *The Guardian*. Available fromhttps://www.theguardian.com/commentisfree/2018/apr/17/france-intervention-syria-macron-french-president-strikes-tony-blair-iraq.

Borger, J. (2012, September 18). Germany Slowly Comes to Terms with Sending Its Armed Forces Abroad. *The Guardian*. https://www.theguardian.com/world/2012/sep/18/germany-military-modernise-foreign-intervention.

Brazier, R. (1999). *Constitutional Reform* (2nd ed.). Oxford: Oxford University Press.

Democratic Audit UK. (2013). *Parliament Has Relatively Weak War Powers Compared to Legislatures in Other Democracies*. Available from http://eprints.lse.ac.uk/81420/1/democraticaudit.com-Parliament%20has%20relatively%20weak%20war%20powers%20compared%20to%20legislatures%20in%20other%20democracies.pdf.

Deutsche Welle. (2010, December 28). *The Balkan Dilemma, Germany Returns to Military Actin*. https://www.dw.com/en/germany-mulls-joining-us-led-airstrikes-in-syria-report/a-45424607.

Deutsche Welle. (2017, September 10). *Germany Mulls Joining US-Led Airstrikes in Syria-Report*. https://www.dw.com/en/germany-mulls-joining-us-led-airstrikes-in-syria-report/a-45424607.

Dieterich, S., Hummel, H., & Marschall, S. (2010). *Parliamentary War Powers: A Survey of 25 European Parliaments, Geneva Centre for the Democratic Control of Armed Forces* (Occasional Paper No. 21). Available from http://www.css.ethz.ch/en/services/digital-library/publications/publication.html/122963.

Fikfak, V., & Hooper, H. (2018). *Whither the War Powers Convention? What Next for Parliamentary Control of Armed Conflict After Syria*. UK Constitutional Law Association. https://ukconstitutionallaw.org/2018/04/20/veronika-fikfak-and-hayley-j-hooper-whither-the-war-powers-convention-what-next-for-parliamentary-control-of-armed-conflict-after-syria/.

HC Deb. (2018, April 17). Vol 639, Col 192–246. Available from https://hansard.parliament.uk/commons/2018-04-17/debates/EF164C0A-E0F5-40B6-A718-DD8693A2490C/MilitaryActionOverseasParliamentaryApproval.

House of Commons. (2006). *Foreign Affairs Committee, Sixth Report*.

ICISS. (2001). *The Responsibility to Protect—Report of the International Commission on Intervention and State Sovereignty*. Ottawa: International Development Research Centre.

Intelligence and Security Committee. (2018). *Report on Detainee Mistreatment and Rendition*. Available from http://isc.independent.gov.uk/committee-reports/special-reports.

Jenkins, D. (2007). Constitutional Reform Goes to War: Some Lessons from the United States. *Public Law*, 258–279.

Mello, P., & Peters, D. (2018). Parliaments in Security Policy: Involvement, Politicisation, and Influence. *The British Journal of Politics and International Relations, 20*(1), 3–18.

Mills, C. (2018). *Parliamentary Approval for Military Action* (Commons Briefing Paper 7166). House of Commons Library.

Ostermann, F. (2017). France's Reluctant Parliamentarisation of Military Deployments: The 2008 Constitutional Reform in Practice. *West European Politics, 40*(2), 101–118.

Raunio, T., & Wagner, W. (2017). Towards Parliamentarisation of Foreign and Security Policy? *West European Politics, 40*(1), 1–19.

Reuters. (2018). *Germany Says in Talks About Possible Military Role in Syria.*

Rogers, P. (2013). Security by "Remote Control": Can It Work? *RUSI Journal, 158*(3), 14–20.

Stein, A. (2018). *Paramilitary Activity: The Unintended Consequences of America's Undeclared War Against Assad.* War on the Rocks. https://warontherocks.com/2018/12/paramilitary-activity-the-unintended-consequences-of-americas-undeclared-war-against-assad/.

Strong, J. (2014). Why Parliament Now Decides on War: Tracing the Growth of the Parliamentary Prerogative Through Syria, Libya an Iraq. *British Journal of Politics and International Relations, 17*(4), 1–19.

Strong, J. (2018). The War Powers of the British Parliament: What Has Been Established and What Remains Unclear. *British Journal of Politics and International Relations, 20,* 19–34.

Wagner, W. (2017). The Bundestag as a Champion of Parliamentary Control of Military Missions. *Security and Peace, 35*(2), 60–65.

Wagner, W., Herranz-Surrallés, A., Kaarbo, J., & Ostermann, F. (2017). The Party Politics of Legislative–Executive Relations in Security and Defence Policy. *West European Politics, 40*(1), 20–41.

Younge, G., & Henley, J. (2003, February 11). *Wimps, Weasels and Monkeys—The US Media View of Perfidious Frances.* https://www.theguardian.com/world/2003/feb/11/pressandpublishing.usa.

Ziegler, K. (2017). 'AWACS I (Ger)'. In R. Grote, R. Wolfrum, & F. Lachenmann (Eds.), *Max Planck Encyclopedia of Comparative Constitutional Law (MPECCoL).*

Ziegler, K. (2019). The Use of Military Force by the United Kingdom, the Evolution of Accountability. In *The Oxford Handbook of Comparative Foreign Relations Law*. Oxford: Oxford University Press.

Bibliography

Abouzeid, R. (2011a, March 24). With Syria on the Brink Assad Promises Reform. *Time*. Available from http://content.time.com/time/world/article/0,8599,2061288,00.html.

Abouzeid, R. (2011b, March 6). Sitting Pretty in Syria: Why Few Go Bashing Bashar. *Time*. Available from http://content.time.com/time/world/article/0,8599,2057067-2,00.html.

AFP/The Local. (2018, April 12). What the Syrian People Want and Need Is Peace and Justice: Swedish Ambassador. *The Local Sweden*. Available from https://www.thelocal.se/20180412/what-the-syrian-people-want-and-need-is-peace-and-justice-sweden-security-council.

Al Jazeera. (2013, November 18). *Obama Signs Secret Order to Aid Syria Rebels*. https://www.aljazeera.com/news/middleeast/2012/08/20128264510724249.html.

Al Jazeera. (2018, April 14). *Syria's War: France Rules Out Confrontation with Russia*. https://www.aljazeera.com/news/2018/04/syria-war-france-rules-confrontation-russia-180414063828974.html.

Allen, G. (2002, September 26). A Degree of Democratic Deficit. *Daily Telegraph*. http://www.telegraph.co.uk/comment/letters/3582038/A-degree-of-democratic-deficit.html.

Amnesty International. (2018). *Syria: US-Led Coalition's Aerial Attacks in Raqqa Killed Hundreds of Civilians*. Available from https://www.amnesty.org.uk/press-releases/syria-us-led-coalitions-aerial-attacks-raqqa-killed-hundreds-civilians-new-report.

Andrews, R. (2004). *Theorising the Third War: Stakeholding, Active Citizenship and Democratic Renewal*. Paper Presented at the PSA Conference,

T. McCormack, *Britain's War Powers*,
https://doi.org/10.1007/978-3-030-13682-6

Lincoln University. Available online at http://www.psa.ac.uk/24journals/pdf/5/2004/Andrews.pdf.

Annan, K. (1999, September 18–24). Two Concepts of Sovereignty. *The Economist*, pp. 81–82.

Ball, J. (2012, August 20). Obama Issues Syria a 'Red Line' Warning on Chemical Weapons. *The Washington Post*. https://www.washingtonpost.com/world/national-security/obama-issues-syria-red-line-warning-on-chemical-weapons/2012/08/20/ba5d26ec-eaf7-11e1-b811-09036bcb182b_story.html?noredirect=on&utm_term=.4fd4eeabaec8.

Bartlett, G., & Everett, M. (2017). *The Royal Prerogative, House of Commons Library* (Briefing Paper No. 03861).

BBC. (undated-a). *The Richard Dimbleby Lecture*. Lord Hailsham: Elective Dictatorship. https://www.bbc.co.uk/programmes/p00fr9gh.

BBC. (undated-b). *Saddam's Iraq: Key Events*. http://news.bbc.co.uk/1/shared/spl/hi/middle_east/02/iraq_events/html/desert_fox.stm.

BBC. (1998). *UK Politics: Talking Politics, Conventions of the Constitution*. http://news.bbc.co.uk/1/hi/uk_politics/88166.stm.

BBC. (2002, September 9). *UN Resolutions on Iraq*. Available from http://news.bbc.co.uk/1/hi/world/middle_east/2246037.stm.

BBC. (2003a, January 15). *Inspectors Search Saddam Palace*. http://news.bbc.co.uk/1/hi/world/middle_east/2660201.stm.

BBC. (2003b, February 16). *'Million' March Against Iraq War*. http://news.bbc.co.uk/1/hi/uk/2765041.stm.

BBC. (2003c, February 21). *UK Tight-Lipped on Iraq Timescale*. http://news.bbc.co.uk/1/hi/uk_politics/2773771.stm.

BBC. (2003d, January 15). *Who's Pressing Blair Against War*. http://news.bbc.co.uk/1/hi/uk_politics/2660957.stm.

BBC. (2003e, March 19). *Blair Wins War Backing Amid Revolt*. http://news.bbc.co.uk/1/hi/uk_politics/2862325.stm.

BBC. (2005, May 27). *Short in Mandatory War Vote Bid*. http://news.bbc.co.uk/1/hi/uk_politics/4585777.stm.

BBC. (2007a, May 15). *MPs Support War-Powers Proposals*. http://news.bbc.co.uk/1/hi/uk_politics/6658161.stm.

BBC. (2007b, July 3). *In Full: Brown on Constitution*. http://news.bbc.co.uk/1/hi/uk_politics/6266526.stm.

BBC. (2011, December 17). *Dr. David Kelly: Controversial Death Examined*. https://www.bbc.co.uk/news/uk-13716127.

BBC. (2013a). https://www.bbc.co.uk/news/uk-21009663.

BBC. (2013b, January 15). *Royal 'Consent' to Laws Revealed After FOI Battle*. Available from https://www.bbc.co.uk/news/uk-politics-21024828.

BBC. (2013c, August 30). *Syria Crisis: Cameron Loses Commons Vote on Syria Action*. Available from http://www.bbc.co.uk/news/uk-politics-23892783.

BBC. (2013d, September 24). *Syria Chemical Attack: What We Know*. https://www.bbc.co.uk/news/world-middle-east-23927399.

BBC. (2014, November 10). *Shaun Ley, How Did the Government Let a Defeat Over Syria Happen*. https://www.bbc.co.uk/news/uk-politics-29985110.

BBC. (2014). https://www.bbc.co.uk/news/uk-politics-26754077.

BBC. (2016a, July 6). *Chilcot Report: What Blair Said to Bush in Memos*. https://www.bbc.co.uk/news/uk-36722312.

BBC. (2016b, August 8). *Quentin Sommerville, UK Special Forces Pictured on the Ground in Syria*. https://www.bbc.co.uk/news/uk-37015915.

BBC. (2018a). *House of Saud, Producer Michael Radford*. Available from https://www.bbc.co.uk/programmes/b09m53py.

BBC. (2018b, April 16). *Syria Air Strikes: Russia Denies Tampering with Suspected Chemical Attack Site*. Available from https://www.bbc.co.uk/news/world-middle-east-43783427.

BBC. (2018c, April 16). *US-Led Strikes on Syria: What Was Hit?* Available from https://www.bbc.co.uk/news/world-middle-east-43769332.

BBC. (2018d, April 14). *Syria Airstrikes the UK Government's Legal Position in Full*. Available from https://www.bbc.co.uk/news/uk-43768145.

Beetham, D. (1991). *The Legitimation of Power*. Basingstoke: Palgrave Macmillan.

Blick, A. (2014). Emergency Powers and the Withering of the Royal Prerogative. *The International Journal of Human Rights, 18*(2), 195–210.

Blunkett, D. (2001). *Politics and Progress: Renewing Democracy and a Civil Society*. London: Demos.

Bock, P. (2018, April 17). Macron's Bid to Look Strong on Syria Could Weaken Him in France. *The Guardian*. Available from-https://www.theguardian.com/commentisfree/2018/apr/17/france-intervention-syria-macron-french-president-strikes-tony-blair-iraq.

Borger, J. (2012, September 18). Germany Slowly Comes to Terms with Sending Its Armed Forces Abroad. *The Guardian*. https://www.theguardian.com/world/2012/sep/18/germany-military-modernise-foreign-intervention.

Bowcott, O. (2016, December 5, Monday). Royal Prerogative Takes Centre Stage as Supreme Court Brexit Case Opens. *The Guardian*. https://www.theguardian.com/politics/2016/dec/05/supreme-court-brexit-case-whose-prerogative-is-it-anyway.

Brazier, R. (1999). *Constitutional Reform* (2nd ed.). Oxford: Oxford University Press.

Brown, C. (2006, June 28). Straw to Call for End to Prime Minister's Royal Prerogative on War. *The Independent*. https://www.independent.co.uk/news/uk/politics/straw-to-call-for-end-to-prime-ministers-royal-prerogative-on-war-6096954.html.

Brown, G., & Straw, J. (2007). *The Governance of Britain, Green Paper*. https://assets.publishing.service.gov.uk/government/uploads/system/uploads/attachment_data/file/228834/7170.pdf.

Burns, R. (2018, April 15). Despite Strikes, Assad Retains Chemical Capability, Pentagon Admits. *The Times of Israel*. Available from https://www.timesofisrael.com/pentagon-despite-strikes-assad-still-has-chemical-weapons/.

Byrne, I., & Weir, S. (2004). Democratic Audit: Executive Democracy in War and Peace. *Parliamentary Affairs, 57*(2), 453–468.

Cabinet Office. (1998). *Your Right to Know: The Government's Proposals for a Freedom of Information Act*. Available from http://www.official-documents.gov.uk/document/cm38/3818/3818.pdf.

Cabinet Office. (2011). *The Cabinet Manual*. Available from https://assets.publishing.service.gov.uk/government/uploads/system/uploads/attachment_data/file/60641/cabinet-manual.pdf.

Chalmers, M. (2013, August 30). *Parliament's Decision on Syria: Pulling Our Punches*. RUSI Analysis. https://rusi.org/commentary/parliaments-decision-syria-pulling-our-punches.

Chappell, B. (2015, September 30). *Russia Begins Airstrikes in Syria After Assad's Request*. National Public Radio. Available from https://www.npr.org/sections/thetwo-way/2015/09/30/444679327/russia-begins-conducting-airstrikes-in-syria-at-assads-request.

Chrisafis, A. (2018, April 10). France Calls for Strong and United Response to Syria Chemical Attack. *The Guardian*. Available from https://www.theguardian.com/world/2018/apr/10/will-emmanuel-macron-enforce-red-line-syria-chemical-attack.

Cook, R. (2003). *The Point of Departure*. New York, NY: Simon & Schuster.

Cooper, H., Gibbons-Neff, T., & Baker, P. (2018, April 12). Mattis Tries to Put Brakes on Possible Syria Strike to 'Keep This From Escalating'. *The New York Times*. Available from https://www.nytimes.com/2018/04/12/us/politics/trump-syria-attack.html.

Crerar, P., & Elgot, J. (2018, April 16). Syria Strikes: May Tells MPs Britain Could Not Wait for UN Approval. *The Guardian*. Available from https://www.theguardian.com/politics/2018/apr/16/syria-strikes-may-tells-mps-uk-could-not-have-waited-for-un-approval.

Democratic Audit, The Federal Trust, & One World Trust. (2006). *Not in Our Name*.

Democratic Audit, The Federal Trust, & One World Trust. (2008). *A World of Difference*.

Democratic Audit UK. (2013). *Parliament Has Relatively Weak War Powers Compared to Legislatures in Other Democracies*. Available from http://eprints.lse.ac.uk/81420/1/democraticaudit.com-Parliament%20has%20relatively%20 weak%20war%20powers%20compared%20to%20legislatures%20in%20other%20democracies.pdf.

Democracy Task Force. (2007). *An End to Sofa Government, Better Working of Prime Minister and Cabine*t. Available from http://image.guardian.co.uk/sys-files/Politics/documents/2007/03/27/DemocracyTaskForce.pdf.

Deutsche Welle. (2010, December 28). *The Balkan Dilemma, Germany Returns to Military Actin.* https://www.dw.com/en/germany-mulls-joining-us-led-airstrikes-in-syria-report/a-45424607.

Deutsche Welle. (2017, September 10). *Germany Mulls Joining US-Led Airstrikes in Syria-Report.* https://www.dw.com/en/germany-mulls-joining-us-led-airstrikes-in-syria-report/a-45424607.

Dicey, A. V. (1962). *Introduction to the Law of the Constitution* (10th ed.). London: Palgrave.

Dieterich, S., Hummel, H., & Marschall, S. (2010). *Parliamentary War Powers: A Survey of 25 European Parliaments, Geneva Centre for the Democratic Control of Armed Forces* (Occasional Paper No. 21). Available from http://www.css.ethz.ch/en/services/digital-library/publications/publication.html/122963.

Driver, S., & Martell, L. (2002). *Blair's Britain.* Cambridge: Polity Press.

DTLGR. (2002). *Your Region, Your Choice: Revitalising the English Regions.* Norwich: Stationery Office.

Edelman, E. S. (2015, August 27). America's Dangerous Bargain with Turkey. *The New York Times.* Available from https://www.nytimes.com/2015/08/27/opinion/americas-dangerous-bargain-with-turkey.html?_r=1.

Elliot, M. (2002). Parliamentary Sovereignty and the New Constitutional Order: Legislative Freedom, Political Reality and Convention. *Legal Studies, 22*(3), 340–375.

Embury-Dennis, T. (2018, April 11). Russia Will Shoot Down Missiles Fired at Syria and Retaliate Against Launch Sites, Says Ambassador. *The Independent.* Available from https://www.independent.co.uk/news/world/middle-east/russia-us-missiles-syria-launch-sites-lebanon-zasypkin-putin-a8298941.html.

Eyal, J. (2013). *Voting for Irrelevance? The UK Parliament Passes Its Verdict.* RUSI Newsbrief. Available from https://www.rusi.org/go.php?structureID=articles_newsbrief&ref=A5225CB57962BB#.VWWhpEuvvFI.

Fikfak, V., & Hooper, H. (2018a). *Parliament's Secret War.* Oxford: Hart.

Fikfak, V., & Hooper, H. (2018b). *Whither the War Powers Convention? What Next for Parliamentary Control of Armed Conflict After Syria.* UK Constitutional Law Association. https://ukconstitutionallaw.org/2018/04/20/veronika-fikfak-and-hayley-j-hooper-whither-the-war-powers-convention-what-next-for-parliamentary-control-of-armed-conflict-after-syria/.

Financial Times. (2013). Isolationism Is Beneath Britain. https://www.ft.com/content/896db8b2-1166-11e3-a14c-00144feabdc0.

Foer, F. (2004, June 7). The Source of the Trouble. *New York Magazine*. http://nymag.com/nymag/9227/.

France 24. (2018, April 14). *A History of the Syria Chemical Weapons 'Red Line'*. https://www.france24.com/en/20180414-syria-chemical-weapons-red-line-obama-macron-assad-russia-usa-france-idlib.

Fukuyama, F. (1992). *The End of History and the Last Man*. New York: The Free Press.

Furedi, F. (2013). *Moral Crusades in an Age of Mistrust, The Jimmy Saville Scandal*. Basingstoke: Palgrave Macmillan.

Gaskarth, J. (2016). The Fiasco of the 2013 Syria Votes: Decline and Denial in British Foreign Policy. *Journal of European Public Policy, 23*(5), 718–734.

Gibbons-Neff, T. (2018, April 19). Missile Strikes Are Unlikely to Stop Syria's Chemical Attacks, Pentagon Says. *The New York Times*.

Giddens, A. (1998). *The Third Way: The Renewal of Social Democracy*. Cambridge: Polity Press.

Giddens, A. 2002. *Where Now for New Labour?* Polity Press: Cambridge.

Gilligan, A. (2013, July 21). The Betrayal of Dr. David Kelly, 10 Years On. *The Daily Telegraph*. https://www.telegraph.co.uk/news/politics/10192271/The-betrayal-of-Dr-David-Kelly-10-years-on.html.

Gray, J., & Lomas, M. (2014). *Who Takes Britain to War?* London: The History Press.

Green, D. A. (2017, April 18). The Fixed Term Parliaments Act Has Failed. *Financial Times*. https://www.ft.com/content/17eda04e-ea24-359a-8c7e-d0caed79cb5e.

Haaretz. (2018, March 28). Saudi Backed Syrian Rebels Face a Stark Choice: Surrender to Assad or Die. *Haaretz*. https://www.haaretz.com/middle-east-news/syria/syrian-army-of-islam-faces-a-stark-choice-surrender-to-assad-or-die-1.5957469.

HC. (2003, March 18). Vol 739, Col 760.

HC. (2011, March 14). Vol 525, Col 38. Available from https://publications.parliament.uk/pa/cm201011/cmhansrd/cm110314/debtext/110314-0001.htm#11031411000731.

HC. (2013, January 31). Vol 557, Col 1059. Available from https://publications.parliament.uk/pa/cm201213/cmhansrd/cm130131/debtext/130131-0001.htm#13013128000706.

HC. (2014, September 26). Vol 585, Col 1265. Available from https://publications.parliament.uk/pa/cm201415/cmhansrd/cm140926/debtext/140926-0001.htm.

HC Deb. (2001, October 8). Vol 372, Col 811. Available from https://publications.parliament.uk/pa/cm200102/cmhansrd/vo011008/debtext/11008-01.htm#11008-01_spmin0%20.

HC Deb. (2007, May 1). Vol 691, Col 979. Available from https://publications.parliament.uk/pa/ld200607/ldhansrd/text/70501-0004.htm#07050146000001.

HC Deb. (2007, May 15). Vol 460, Col 481. Available from https://publications.parliament.uk/pa/cm200607/cmhansrd/cm070515/debindx/70515-x.htm.

HC Deb. (2011, February 28). Vol 524, Col 24. Available from https://publications.parliament.uk/pa/cm201011/cmhansrd/cm110228/debtext/110228-0001.htm#11022819000002.

HC Deb. (2011, March 10). Vol 524, Col 1066. Available from https://publications.parliament.uk/pa/cm201011/cmhansrd/cm110310/debtext/110310-0001.htm.

HC Deb. (2011, March 21). Vol 527, Col 700–801. Available from https://publications.parliament.uk/pa/cm201011/cmhansrd/cm110321/debtext/110321-0002.htm.

HC Deb. (2013, August 29). Vol 566, Col 1425. Available from https://publications.parliament.uk/pa/cm201314/cmhansrd/cm130829/debtext/130829-0001.htm.

HC Deb. (2018, April 16). Vol 639, Col 39–92. Available from https://hansard.parliament.uk/Commons/2018-04-16/debates/92610F86-2B91-4105-AE8B-78D018453D1B/Syria.

HC Deb. (2018, April 17). Vol 639, Col 192–246. Available from https://hansard.parliament.uk/commons/2018-04-17/debates/EF164C0A-E0F5-40B6-A718-DD8693A2490C/MilitaryActionOverseasParliamentaryApproval.

HC Written Statement. (2016, April 18). HCWS678. Available from https://www.parliament.uk/written-questions-answers-statements/written-statement/Commons/2016-04-18/HCWS678.

HL Deb. (2007, May 1). Vol 691, Col 979. Available from https://publications.parliament.uk/pa/ld200607/ldhansrd/index/070501.html#contents.

HL Written Answers. (2018, April 16). HL6958. Available from https://www.parliament.uk/business/publications/written-questions-answers-statements/written-question/Lords/2018-04-16/HL6958/.

HL Written Answers. (2018, April 17). HL7011. Available from https://www.parliament.uk/business/publications/written-questions-answers-statements/written-question/Lords/2018-04-17/HL7011/.

Hansard Society. (2012). *Audit of Political Engagement 9*. London: Hansard Society. Available online at http://www.hansardsociety.org.uk/blogs/press_releases/archive/2012/04/25/audit-of-political-engagement-9-part-one.aspx.

Hegemann, H. (2018). Toward 'Normal' Politics? Security, Parliaments and the Politicisation of Intelligence Oversight in the German Bundestag. *The British Journal of Politics and International Relations, 20*(1), 175–190.

Hehir, A. (2013). The Permanence of Inconsistency: Libya, the Security Council, and the Responsibility to Protect. *International Security, 38*(1), 137–159.

Herbel, A. (2016). Parliamentary scrutiny of the EU's Common Foreign and Security Policy. *West European Politics, 40*(1), 161–182.

Houeix, R. (2018, April 16). *A History of the Syria Chemical Weapons 'Red Line'*. France 24. Available from http://www.france24.com/en/20180414-syria-chemical-weapons-red-line-obama-macron-assad-russia-usa-france-idlib.

House of Commons. (2000). *Foreign Affairs Committee, Fourth Report, Kosovo*. Available fromhttps://publications.parliament.uk/pa/cm199900/cmselect/cmfaff/28/2802.htm.

House of Commons. (2004). Public Administration Select Committee, *Taming the Royal Prerogative: Strengthening Ministerial Accountability to Parliament*. Fourth Report Session 2003–04, HC 422.

House of Commons. (2006). *Foreign Affairs Committee, Sixth Report*.

House of Commons. (2008). Public Administration Select Committee First Report, *Constitutional Renewal: Draft Bill and White Paper*. Tenth Report of Session 2007–08 HC 499.

House of Commons. (2010). Public Administration Select Committee, *Who Does UK National Strategy*. First Report of Session 2010–11, HC 435.

House of Commons. (2011a). Political and Constitutional Reform Committee, *Parliament's Role in Conflict Decisions*. Eight Report of Session 2010–12, HC 923.

House of Commons. (2011b). Political and Constitutional Reform Committee, *Parliament's Role in Conflict Decisions, Further Government Response*. Twelfth Report of Session 2010–12, HC 1673.

House of Commons. (2013). Political and Constitutional Reform Committee, *Parliament's Role in Conflict Decisions: An Update*. Eight Report of Session 2013–14.

House of Commons. (2014a). Political and Constitutional Reform Committee, *Parliament's Role in Conflict Decisions: A Way Forward*. Twelfth Report of Session 2013–14, HC 892.

House of Commons. (2014b). Political and Constitutional Reform Committee, *Role and Powers of the Prime Minister*. First Report of Session 2014–15, HC 351.

House of Commons. (2015). Political and Constitutional Reform Committee, *Revisiting the Cabinet Manual*. Fifth Report of Session 2014–15.

House of Commons. (2016). Foreign Affairs Committee, *Libya: Examination of Intervention and Collapse and the UK's Future Policy Options*. Third Report of Session 2016–17, HC 119.

House of Commons. (2018a, April 16). *Syria Debate.* https://hansard.parliament.uk/Commons/2018-04-16/debates/92610F86-2B91-4105-AE8B-78D018453D1B/Syria.

House of Commons. (2018b, April 17). *Military Action Overseas, Parliamentary Approval Debate.* https://hansard.parliament.uk/Commons/2018-04-17/debates/EF164C0A-E0F5-40B6-A718-DD8693A2490C/MilitaryActionOverseasParliamentaryApproval.

House of Commons Library Research Library. (2008). *Parliamentary Approval for Deploying the Armed Forces.*

House of Lords. (2004). Select Committee on the Constitution, *Parliament and the Legislative Process.* 14th Report of Session 2003–4, HL Paper 173-I.

House of Lords. (2006). Select Committee on the Constitution, *Waging War: Parliament's Role and Responsibility.* 15th Report of Session 2005–06, HL Paper 236-I.

House of Lords. (2007). Select Committee on the Constitution, *Waging War: Parliament's Role and Responsibility, Follow Up.* Report 15th Report of Session 2006–07, HL Paper 51.

House of Lords. (2013). Constitution Committee, *Second Report, Constitutional Arrangements for the Use of Force.* HL Paper 46.

House of Lords, House of Commons. (2006a). Joint Committee on Conventions, *Conventions of the UK Parliament.* First Report of Session 2005–06, HL Paper 265-I, HC 1212-I.

House of Lords, House of Commons. (2006b). Joint Committee on the Draft Constitutional Renewal Bill, Session 2007–08, HL Paper 166-I HC Paper 551-I.

House of Lords, House of Commons (2008). Joint Committee on the Draft Constitutional Renewal Bill, Session 2007–08, HL Paper 166-I HC Paper 551-I.

Howell, W., & Pevehouse, J. (2007). *While Dangers Gather: Congressional Checks on Presidential War Powers.* Princeton: Princeton University Press.

Hudson, V. (2013). *Foreign Policy Analysis: Classic and Contemporary Theory.* London: Rowman and Littlefield.

Hutton, W. (1997). An Overview of Stakeholding. In G. Kelly, D. Kelly, & A. Gamble (Eds.), *Stakeholder Capitalism* (pp. 3–9). Basingstoke: Palgrave Macmillan.

ICISS. (2001). *The Responsibility to Protect—Report of the International Commission on Intervention and State Sovereignty.* Ottawa: International Development Research Centre.

Intelligence and Security Committee. (2018). *Report on Detainee Mistreatment and Rendition.* Available from http://isc.independent.gov.uk/committee-reports/special-reports.

Iraq Inquiry. (2016). *The Report of the Iraq Inquiry*. Available from http://webarchive.nationalarchives.gov.uk/20171123123237/http://www.iraqinquiry.org.uk/.

Jacobs, P. (2018, April 14). The US Says It Didn't Give Russia Any Advance Warning About Targets Hit in Syria Strikes. *Business Insider UK*. http://uk.businessinsider.com/us-russia-syria-strike-targets-no-advance-warning-2018-4?r=US&IR=T.

Jaconelli, J. (1999). The Nature of Constitutional Convention. *Legal Studies, 19*(1), 24–46.

Jenkins, D. (2007). Constitutional Reform Goes to War: Some Lessons from the United States. *Public Law*, 258–279.

Jones, G. (2006, February 6). Cameron Seeks to Limit Blair's Use of Royal Prerogative. *The Daily Telegraph*. https://www.telegraph.co.uk/news/uknews/1509778/Cameron-seeks-to-limit-Blairs-use-of-Royal-Prerogative.html.

Joseph, R. (2013). *The War Prerogative: History, Reform, and Constitutional Design*. Oxford: Oxford University Press.

Kaarbo, J. (2015). A Foreign Policy Analysis Perspective on the Domestic Politics Turn in IR Theory. *International Studies Review, 17*(2), 189–216.

Kaarbo, J. (2018). Prime Minister Leadership Style and the Role of Parliament in Security Policy. *The British Journal of Politics and International Relations, 20*(1), 35–51.

Kaarbo, J., & Kenealy, D. (2016). No, Prime Minister: Explaining the House of Commons' Vote on Intervention in Syria. *European Security, 25*(1), 28–48.

Kesgin, B., & Kaarbo, J. (2010). When and How Parliaments Influence Foreign Policy: The Case of Turkey's Iraq Decision. *International Studies Perspectives, 11*(1), 19–36.

Kheel, R. (2018, April 13). Mattis Resists Trump's Calls for Larger Syrian Strike: Report. *The Hill*. Available from http://thehill.com/policy/defense/383107-mattis-halted-two-opportunities-to-strike-syria-this-week-report.

Lagassé, P. (2017). Parliament and the War Prerogative in the United Kingdom and Canada: Explaining Variations in Institutional Change and Legislative Control. *Parliamentary Affairs, 70*(2), 280–300.

Lagasse, P., & Saideman, S. (2017). Public Critic or Secretive Monitor: Party Objectives and Legislative Oversight of the Military in Canada. *West European Politics, 40*(1), 119–138.

Lockie, A. (2018, April 12). Trump Will Reportedly Warn Russia Where in Syria the US Will Strike. *Business Insider UK*. http://uk.businessinsider.com/trump-will-reportedly-warn-russia-where-us-will-strike-in-syria-2018-4?r=US&IR=T.

MacAskill, E., & Cobain, I. (2014, February 11). British Forces' Century of Unbroken Warfare Set to End with Afghanistan Exit. *The Guardian*.

Mair, P. (2013). *Ruling the Void: The Hollowing of Western Democracy*. London: Verso.

Marshall, G. (1985). What Are Constitutional Conventions? *Parliamentary Affairs, 38*(1), 33–39.

Mazzetti, M., Goldman, A., & Schmidt, M. (2017, August 2). Behind the Sudden Death of a $1 Billion Secret CIA War in Syria. *The New York Times*. https://www.nytimes.com/2017/08/02/world/middleeast/cia-syria-rebel-arm-train-trump.html.

McCormack, T. (2014). The British National Security Strategy: Security After Representation. *British Journal of Politics and International Relations, 17*(3), 494–511.

McCormack, T. (2016). The Emerging Parliamentary Convention on British Military Action and Warfare by Remote Control. *The RUSI Journal, 161*(2), 22–29.

McGregor, R., & Aglionby, J. (2013, August 29). Cameron Loses Commons Syria Vote. *Financial Times*. Available from https://www.ft.com/content/b16c699c-1096-11e3-b291-00144feabdc0.

McHarg, A. (2008). Reforming the United Kingdom Constitution: Law, Convention, Soft Law. *The Modern Law Review, 71*(6), 853–877.

Mello, P. (2017). Curbing the Royal Prerogative to Use Military Force: The British House of Commons and the Conflicts in Libya and Syria. *West European Politics, 40*(1), 80–100.

Mello, P., & Peters, D. (2018). Parliaments in Security Policy: Involvement, Politicisation, and Influence. *The British Journal of Politics and International Relations, 20*(1), 3–18.

Mills, C. (2014). *Parliamentary Approval for Deploying the Armed Forces, An Update* (Standard Note SN05908). House of Commons Library.

Mills, C. (2018). *Parliamentary Approval for Military Action* (Commons Briefing Paper 7166). House of Commons Library.

Ministry of Justice. (2007). *The Governance of Britain: War Powers and Treaties: Limiting Executive Powers*. Cm 7239.

Ministry of Justice. (2008). *The Governance of Britain: Constitutional Renewal*. Cm 7342-I.

Moylan, J. (2012, September 7). *Union Membership Has Halved Since 1980*. BBC. Available online at http://www.bbc.co.uk/news/business-19521535.

Nambiar, S. (1999). NATO Celebrates Its Fiftieth Anniversary by Destroying Yugoslavia. *Mediterranean Quarterly, 10*(3), 15–24.

NBC News. (2005, April 25). *CIA's Final Report: No WMD Found in Iraq*. http://www.nbcnews.com/id/7634313/ns/world_news-mideast_n_africa/t/cias-final-report-no-wmd-found-iraq/#.XBlay8acY_V.

Newman, J. (2005). Enter the Transformational Leader: Network Governance and the Micropolitics of Modernization. *Sociology, 39*(4), 717–734.

Norton-Taylor, R. (2016, April 18). Ministers Drop Plans for War Powers Law. *The Guardian*. Available from https://www.theguardian.com/politics/2016/apr/18/ministers-abandon-plan-war-powers-law-mps-troops.

OPCW. (2018, April 10). *OPCW Will Deploy Fact-Finding Mission to Douma, Syria*. Available from https://www.opcw.org/news/article/opcw-will-deploy-fact-finding-mission-to-douma-syria/.

Ostermann, F. (2017). France's Reluctant Parliamentarisation of Military Deployments: The 2008 Constitutional Reform in Practice. *West European Politics, 40*(2), 101–118.

OUP. (2000). *The Kosovo Report, The Independent International Commission on Kosovo*. Oxford.

Payne, S. (2008). War Powers the War Prerogative and Constitutional Change. *The RUSI Journal, 153*(3), 28–35.

Peters, D., & Wagner, W. (2011). Between Military Efficiency and Democratic Legitimacy: Mapping Parliamentary War Powers in Contemporary Democracies, 1989–2004. *Parliamentary Affairs, 64*(2), 175–192.

Phillipson, G. (2013, September 19). *Historic' Commons' Syria Vote: The Constitutional Significance (Part I)*. UK Const. L. Blog. Available at http://ukconstitutionallaw.org.

Phillipson, G. (2014). *Parliament's Role in the Use of Military Action After the Syria Vote*. Vimeo. https://vimeo.com/88916249.

Power Inquiry. (2006). *Power to the People: The Report of Power: An Independent Enquiry into Britain's Democracy*. York: The Power Inquiry.

Prime Minister's Office. (2017). *Conservative and DUP Agreement and UK Government Financial Support for Northern Ireland*. Available from https://www.gov.uk/government/publications/conservative-and-dup-agreement-and-uk-government-financial-support-for-northern-ireland.

Radice, G. (Ed.). (1996). *What Needs to Change*. London: HarperCollins.

Ramsay, P. (2012). *The Insecurity State, Vulnerable Autonomy and the Right to Security in the Criminal Law*. Oxford: Oxford University Press.

Raunio, T. (2016). Refusing to Be Sidelined: The Engagement of the Finnish Eduskunta in Foreign Affairs. *Scandinavian Political Studies, 39*(4), 312–332.

Raunio, T. (2018). Parliament as an Arena for Politicisation: The Finnish Eduskunta and Crisis Management Operations. *The British Journal of Politics and International Relations, 20*(1), 158–174.

Raunio, T., & Wagner, W. (2017). Towards Parliamentarisation of Foreign and Security Policy? *West European Politics, 40*(1), 1–19.

Rayner, G., Riley-Smith, B., & Luhn, A. (2018, April 13). US-Russia 'Hotline' for Syrian Airstrikes Could Help Avoid Conflict Esclating. *The Telegraph*. https://www.telegraph.co.uk/news/2018/04/12/us-russia-hotline-syrian-air-strikes-could-help-avoid-conflict/.

Reuters. (2011, August 22). *Timeline: Libya's Uprising Against Muammar Gaddafi.* https://www.reuters.com/article/us-libya-events-idUSTRE77K2QH20110822.

Reuters. (2018a, March 12). *Syrian Observatory Says War Has Killed More Than Half a Million.* Available from https://www.reuters.com/article/us-mid-east-crisis-syria/syrian-observatory-says-war-has-killed-more-than-half-a-million-idUSKCN1GO13M.

Reuters. (2018b, April 8). *Syria Says Ready to Start Rebel Talks After Alleged Gas Attack.* Available from https://www.reuters.com/article/us-mideast-crisis-syria-ghouta/syria-says-ready-to-start-rebel-talks-after-alleged-gas-attack-idUSKBN1HF074.

Reuters. (2018c, April 14). *Pro-Assad Official Says Targeted Bases Were Evacuated on Russian Warning.* Available from https://www.reuters.com/article/us-mideast-crisis-syria-assessment/pro-assad-official-says-targeted-bases-were-evacuated-on-russian-warning-idUSKBN1HL07R.

Reuters. (2018d). *Germany Says in Talks About Possible Military Role in Syria.*

Rogers, P. (2013). Security by "Remote Control": Can It Work? *RUSI Journal, 158*(3), 14–20.

Rosén, G., & Raube, K. (2018). Influence Beyond Formal Powers: The Parliamentarisation of EU Security Policy. *The British Journal of Politics and International Relations, 20*(1), 69–83.

Ross, T. (2011, July 8). Church of England Faces Being Wiped Out, Report Warns. *The Daily Telegraph.* Available online at http://www.telegraph.co.uk/news/religion/8626410/Church-of-England-faces-being-wiped-out-report-warns.html.

Schmitt, E. (2016, November 21). *ISIS Used Chemical Arms at Least 52 Times in Syria and Iraq, Report Says.* https://www.nytimes.com/2016/11/21/world/middleeast/isis-chemical-weapons-syria-iraq-mosul.html.

Schuster, J., & Maier, H. (2006). The Rift: Explaining Europe's Divergent Iraq Policies in the Run-Up of the American-Led War on Iraq. *Foreign Policy Analysis, 2*(3), 223–244.

Shaheen, K. (2018, April 8). *Dozens Killed in Suspected Chemical Attack on Syrian Rebel Enclave.* Available from https://www.theguardian.com/world/2018/apr/08/syrian-government-accused-of-chemical-attacks-on-civilians-in-eastern-ghouta.

Sky News. (2018, April 21). *Russia: We Told US Where in Syria They Could Not Bomb.* Available from https://news.sky.com/story/russia-we-told-us-where-in-syria-they-could-not-bomb-11338625.

Sparrow, A., & Perraudin, F. (2015, December 3). Cameron Wins Syria Airstrikes Vote by Majority of 174—As It Happened. *The Guardian.* Available from https://www.theguardian.com/politics/blog/live/2015/dec/02/syria-airstrikes-mps-debate-vote-cameron-action-against-isis-live.

Stein, A. (2018). *Paramilitary Activity: The Unintended Consequences of America's Undeclared War Against Assad*. War on the Rocks. https://warontherocks.com/2018/12/paramilitary-activity-the-unintended-consequences-of-americas-undeclared-war-against-assad/.

Sterling, R. (2005). Promoting Democratic Governance Through Partnerships? In J. Newman (Ed.), *Remaking Governance: Peoples, Politics and the Public Sphere*. Bristol: The Policy Press.

Stevenson, A. (2013, January 15). *Still Powerful, Still an Accountable: Full Extent of Royal Veto Power Revealed*. http://www.politics.co.uk/news/2013/01/15/still-powerful-still-unaccountable-full-extent-of-royal-veto.

Straw, J. (1994). Abolish the Royal Prerogative. In A. Barnett (Ed.), *Power and the Throne: The Monarchy Debate* (pp. 125–129). London: Vintage.

Strong, J. (2014). Why Parliament Now Decides on War: Tracing the Growth of the Parliamentary Prerogative Through Syria, Libya an Iraq. *British Journal of Politics and International Relations, 17*(4), 1–19.

Strong, J. (2018). The War Powers of the British Parliament: What Has Been Established and What Remains Unclear. *British Journal of Politics and International Relations, 20*, 19–34.

Sylvester, R., & Thomson, A. (2005, April 30). Brown: I Would Give MPs Last Word on War. *The Daily Telegraph*. https://www.telegraph.co.uk/news/uknews/1488989/Brown-I-would-give-MPs-last-word-on-war.html.

TASS. (2017, December 27). *Russian Military Advisors Work with All Syrian Army Units—Russian General Staff*. Available from http://tass.com/world/983232.

Taylor, C., & Kelly, R. (2008). *Parliamentary Approval for Deploying the Armed Forces: An Introduction to the Issues* (Research Paper 08/08). House of Commons Library.

Tempest, M. (2003, March 18). Parliament Gives Blair Go-Ahead for War. *The Guardian*. https://www.theguardian.com/politics/2003/mar/18/iraq.iraq6.

Tempest, M. (2005, August 11). *Inquiry to Look at MPs' Role in Declaring War*. https://www.theguardian.com/politics/2005/aug/11/houseofcommons.uk.

UN. (1991, April 5). *UNSCR 688*. Available at http://unscr.com/en/resolutions/688.

UN. (2011, March 17). *Security Council 6498th Meeting, SC/10200*. https://www.un.org/press/en/2011/sc10200.doc.htm.

UN. (2018, April 10). *Security Council 8228th Meeting, SC/13288*. Available from https://www.un.org/press/en/2018/sc13288.doc.htm.

UNHCR. (2018). *Syria Emergency*. Available from http://www.unhcr.org/uk/syria-emergency.html.

United Nations Security Council Resolution 1368. Available from http://unscr.com/en/resolutions/1368.

Vasquez, M., & Hansler, J. (2018, April 12). *Trump Taunts Russia, Says US Military Response Coming in Syria*. CNN. Available from https://edition.cnn.com/2018/04/11/politics/trump-missiles-tweet/index.html.

Veselinovic, M., & Vonberg, J. (2018, April 13). *Syrian Regime 'Highly Likely' to Blame for Chemical Attack, UK Says*. CNN. Available from https://edition.cnn.com/2018/04/12/middleeast/uk-france-support-us-syria-airstrikes-intl/index.html.

Wagner, W. (2006). The Democratic Control of Military Power Europe. *Journal of European Public Policy, 13*(2), 200–216.

Wagner, W. (2017). The Bundestag as a Champion of Parliamentary Control of Military Missions. *Security and Peace, 35*(2), 60–65.

Wagner, W. (2018). Is There a Parliamentary Peace? Parliamentary Veto Power and Military Interventions from Kosovo to Daesh. *The British Journal of Politics and International Relations, 20*(1), 121–134.

Wagner, W., Peters, D., & Glahn, C. (2010). *Parliamentary War Powers Around the World, 1989–2004: A New Dataset* (Occasional Paper No. 22). Geneva: Centre for the Democratic Control of Armed Forces (DCAF).

Wagner, W., Herranz-Surrallés, A., Kaarbo, J., & Ostermann, F. (2017). The Party Politics of Legislative–Executive Relations in Security and Defence Policy. *West European Politics, 40*(1), 20–41.

Walker, J. (2018, April 12). Theresa May Told She Must Ask Parliament Before UK Joins Attack on Syria. *Chronical Live*. Available from https://www.chroniclelive.co.uk/news/north-east-news/theresa-told-must-ask-parliament-14524618.

Walpole, L., & Karlshoej-Pedersen, M. (2018). *Britain's Shadow Army: Policy Options for External Oversight of UK Special Forces*. Oxford Research Group, Remote Warfare Programme. Available from http://www.oxfordresearchgroup.org.uk/sites/default/files/Shadow%20Army%20Policy%20Report_%20PDF.pdf.

Ware, R. (2018, April 16). *The Legal Basis for Air Strikes Against Syrian Government Targets* (House of Commons Library Briefing Paper No. 8287).

Whiteley, P. (2011). *Political Participation in Britain*. London: Palgrave.

Wilson, R. (2004). The Robustness of Conventions in a Time of Modernisation and Change. *Public Law* (Summer), 407–420.

Wintour, P., & Watt, N. (2015, September 7). UK Forces Kill British Isis Fighters in Targeted Drone Strike on Syrian City. *The Guardian*. https://www.theguardian.com/uk-news/2015/sep/07/uk-forces-airstrike-killed-isis-briton-reyaad-khan-syria.

YouGov. (2014). *Report on British Attitudes to Defence, Security and the Armed Forces, Survey Results Pages 6–10*. Available from http://cdn.yougov.com/cumulus_uploads/document/uv4r28gl4x/B_DEFSEC_2.pdf.

YouGov. (2018, April 12). *By Two to One, the Public Oppose Missile Strikes on Syria*. Available from https://yougov.co.uk/news/2018/04/12/two-one-public-oppose-missile-strikes-syria/.

Younge, G., & Henley, J. (2003, February 11). *Wimps, Weasels and Monkeys—The US Media View of Perfidious Frances*. https://www.theguardian.com/world/2003/feb/11/pressandpublishing.usa.

Zenko, M. (2016). *The Big Lie About the Libyan War, Foreign Policy*. Available from http://foreignpolicy.com/2016/03/22/libya-and-the-myth-of-humanitarian-intervention/.

Ziegler, K. (2017). 'AWACS I (Ger)'. In R. Grote, R. Wolfrum, & F. Lachenmann (Eds.), *Max Planck Encyclopedia of Comparative Constitutional Law (MPECCoL)*.

Ziegler, K. (2019). The Use of Military Force by the United Kingdom, the Evolution of Accountability. In *The Oxford Handbook of Comparative Foreign Relations Law*. Oxford: Oxford University Press.

The manufacturer's authorised representative in the EU is Springer Nature Customer Service Centre GmbH, Europaplatz 3, 69115 Heidelberg, Germany. If you have any concerns regarding our products, please contact ProductSafety@springernature.com

Printed and bound by CPI Group (UK) Ltd, Croydon, CR0 4YY
25/09/2026
02222890-0011